A Stranger in My Own Country

Khadim Hussain Raja

A Stranger in My Own Country
East Pakistan, 1969–1971

Major General (Retd.)
KHADIM HUSSAIN RAJA

Introduction by
Muhammad Reza Kazimi

The University Press Limited

The University Press Limited
Red Crescent House
61 Motijheel C/A, P.O. Box 2611
Dhaka 1000, Bangladesh
Phones: (8802) 9565441, 9565444
e-mail: upl@bangla.net, info@uplbooks.com.bd
website: www.uplbooks.com.bd

Bangladesh edition 2012

First published 2012

Copyright © Oxford University Press, Pakistan 2012

The moral rights of the author have been asserted

All rights are reserved. No part of this publication may be reproduced or transmitted in any form or by any means without prior permission in writing from the publisher. Any person who does any unauthorized act in relation to this publication shall be liable to criminal prosecution and civil claims for damages.

Published under a special arrangement with Oxford University Press Pakistan. This edition is licensed for sale in Bangladesh only.

Cover design: *Author's sketch courtesy Saeed Akhtar*

ISBN 978 984 506 116 2

Published by The University Press Limited, Red Crescent House, 61 Motijheel Commercial Area, Dhaka-1000 and printed at the Akota Offset Press, 119 Fakirapool, Dhaka, Bangladesh.

To

RAFIA

"I was most fortunate in having him as my principal subordinate during a critical, historical and tragic period in East Pakistan. His qualities of character and leadership were a great asset. Nor can I forget his personal fidelity and professional distinction."

Sahabzada Yaqub Khan

I had known Khadim Hussain since we served together in the same Brigade HQ in Burma, and later in Siam. We were also on the Directing Staff of the Staff College and I considered myself very fortunate in having him. An impressive personality with all the right instincts, not very articulate in speech, but everything he did was first-class. He had the ability to carry out the three Fs—Firm, Friendly, and Fair. Under his guidance, the HQ soon pulsated with life.

> **Lieutenant General (Retd.) M. Attiqur Rahman**
> *Back to the Pavilion*
> Karachi: Oxford University Press, 2005, pp. 132–3

A soft-spoken and very capable officer he rose rapidly in the army hierarchy. In his death we have lost a quiet but highly regarded and illustrious gunner officer, and a very considerate person.

> **Colonel (Retd.) E.A.S. Bokhari**
> *Defence Journal*
> http://www.defencejournal.com/2000/jan/obituary.htm

Contents

Introduction by Muhammad Reza Kazimi ... xiii

1. The Brewing Storm ... 1
2. Prelude to the 1970 Elections ... 13
3. The Rising Sun of the Awami League ... 28
4. The Devastating Cyclone of November 1970 ... 36
5. A No-Win Situation ... 40
6. The Crisis Deepens ... 46
7. Lt. Gen. Tikka Khan in Action ... 64
8. Operation Searchlight ... 78
9. Last Words… ... 100

Annexure A: Extract of Article by Rehman Sobhan, *South Asian Review*, London, July 1971 ... 112
Annexure B: Operational Details of 'Operation Searchlight' ... 114
Annexure C: Recommendations Regarding Military Operations, 11 April 1971 ... 123

Index ... 127

Introduction
By Muhammad Reza Kazimi

History, it is often said, 'is written by victors'. In the case of East Pakistan, it has been written by the losers. One general,[1] one lieutenant general,[2] four major generals,[3] and two brigadiers[4] have given their account of the events leading to the secession of East Pakistan. Some of their compatriots, who witnessed or participated in the event, are still reluctant to publish their impressions. The credibility of such accounts depends on whether they were written for self-justification or for introspection. The utility of such accounts depends on whether they are relevant. On both counts, these recollections of the late Major General Khadim Hussain Raja are of definite value. They are candid and revealing; they are also imbued with respect for the opposite point of view. He does not fully endorse, but offers for our consideration, a parallel study by the Bengali economist, Rehman Sobhan. These recollections were recorded before, but are being published after the release of the Hamoodur Rahman Commission Report.[5]

It is a tribute to the honesty and perception of Khadim Hussain Raja that *A Stranger in My Own Country* is still of interest to the citizens of Pakistan, India, and Bangladesh; though it is of special worth and utility for the people of Pakistan who need to distinguish between the structural and incidental causes of alienation and separation. The most-favoured explanation for the separation in Pakistan is simple and remorseful: We exploited East Pakistan and, when the people rose demanding their right of self-determination, the Pakistan military, then in power, retaliated with genocide. It served Pakistan right that Bangladesh seceded!

However, history acquires meaning only if we are able to derive a principle from its events, for a principle can be applied to unfolding events to assess their likely outcome. Should we conclude then, from the above explanation of the split, that all people who are exploited or tyrannized acquire the right to self-determination? Bangladesh is the only country, after the Second World War, to succeed in its bid to secede. Thus, we have to search for the uncommon factor between Bangladesh, Palestine, and Chechnya. If we mention Indian armed intervention as the overriding uncommon factor, we shall be banal. It is not the fact that India took advantage of our internal dissensions that invites introspection, but the factors contributing to those dissensions.

It is in identifying such factors that Khadim Hussain Raja has made his momentous contribution. Apart from his direct narration of the events, his portrayal of the major dramatis personae is insightful. These are Field Marshal Mohammad Ayub Khan, General Agha Mohammad Yahya Khan, Lieutenant General Tikka Khan, and Lieutenant General A.A.K. Niazi.

The author records the ire of Ayub Khan, when he was reassuring him that the opposition in Pakistan was of little consequence (p. 3). This was at a time when the vital need was for democracy. Khadim Hussain Raja's estimate was not merely personal. He recalls that Indian pilgrims, during the

Haj, warned him that the agitation against Ayub Khan was a grave error, and that the people of Pakistan would regret their emotional outburst (p. 8). The people were agitating for democracy but what they achieved was instability and dismemberment. Events proved the Indian pilgrims right. Are we then to conclude that outsiders have a clearer view of events than those who flow with them?

The greatest temptation is to subscribe to a stand that has been vindicated, but the real question to pose is whether Ayub Khan's survival in power would have led to the retention of the eastern wing. It would not; and, while Khadim Hussain Raja records the Indian advice, he does not subscribe to it. The option was not of making a choice between stability and world respect on the one hand, and abstract principles like democracy on the other; the people of Pakistan were not agitating with one voice, but only against a single ruler. The agitation in West Pakistan was against the Tashkent Declaration[6] and, in East Pakistan, for the implementation of the Six Points.[7] The divergence, which led to dismemberment, was already there.

Khadim Hussain Raja has not left our question unanswered. Ayub Khan had made a grave error of judgement in thinking that the opposition was of little consequence. He underlines this by recounting how Ataur Rahman asked, long before the crackdown, when the '"West Pakistan Army of Occupation" would leave East Pakistan' (p. 17). It surfaces that the opposition was gathering strength because it was being sidelined.

Khadim Hussain Raja admits freely that: 'In a totalitarian regime, only the person at the top can take momentous and important decisions that are called for' (p. 56). In his portrayal of Yahya Khan, Khadim Hussain Raja places emphasis on not the hierarchical, but the personalized nature of Yahya's regime. A military regime has a chain of command which, if never democratic, is nevertheless efficient. Khadim Hussain Raja has shown how Yahya Khan's debauchery broke even the command chain. He attempts no defence of Yahya's moral character: 'too disgraceful to be put into print' (p. 23). This resulted in senior and responsible officers, like Lieutenant General Yaqub Khan and Admiral S.M. Ahsan, being denied access to the President. Yahya Khan's gullibility, with regard to the significance of the Six Points, could have been possible only in a crony-insulated situation and not within a disciplined military command. This was a medieval milieu and received a medieval response. Foreign intervention by itself, as we proposed earlier, did not constitute the uncommon factor.

Khadim Hussain Raja wrongs Yahya Khan just once, when he accuses him of arbitrarily undoing One Unit[8] and inter-wing parity. On both these counts, a political consensus had already developed in both the wings. Nevertheless, Khadim Hussain Raja is most pertinent when he laments that one whole year was allowed for the electoral campaign. The Legal Framework Order[9] was drafted in a drift, and acquired a major flaw, in the sense that a two-thirds majority—almost a universal convention—was not made a condition for framing of the Constitution. The 120-days limit placed on the Constituent Assembly, to produce a constitution on pain of dissolution, was one of the most inane provisions that could have been imagined. To this slovenly attitude, described by Khadim Hussain Raja, must be added his observation that Yahya's advisers had tried to use money and influence against the Awami League, but these attempts were so crude that they produced the opposite results (p. 22).

This belies the impression that the Yahya regime had given an open field to the Awami League during the elections. This is the reason why the regime thought no political party would emerge with an outright majority.

The two other major players receiving Khadim Hussain Raja's attention are Lieutenant General A.A.K. Niazi and Lieutenant General Tikka Khan. He needs only two strokes to portray Niazi. Niazi threatened to rape Bengali women, causing a Bengali officer of the Pakistan army to leave the room immediately and shoot himself (p. 97). This act apparently left Niazi unmoved because, the next day, brushing aside discussion about the ongoing conflict, he asked Raja for the phone numbers of his 'girl friends' (p. 98). Tikka Khan's venality is clearly apparent but, still, it was because of his temperament that the crisis exacerbated. Disregarding Khadim Hussain Raja's advice that Sheikh Mujibur Rahman be flown out in secrecy, Tikka Khan spoke of trying and hanging Sheikh Mujibur Rahman, right there in Dhaka!

As for the stages in which the crisis unfolded, Khadim Hussain Raja does not take sides. While he blames the outbreak of violence on the Awami League, he also makes it abundantly clear that Yahya Khan had decided upon military action in January/February 1971, in advance of the 1 March 1971 outbreak of violence. This decision seems to be one of the shadows which overcast the tripartite conference between Yahya Khan, Sheikh Mujibur Rahman, and Zulfikar Ali Bhutto.

Khadim Hussain Raja decries the crisis of legitimacy, as also the constitutional vacuum, which enabled the crisis to overflow international frontiers. He strongly disapproves of the moral lapses; he notes the deep-seated ethnic prejudice that had gathered momentum once the patriotic fervour of the 1965 war had abated; but, as the underlying and crucial cause of the debacle, he focuses on the denial of opportunity, a feature inherent in autocratic rule: 'The historic example of the independent state of Pakistan was too recent to be forgotten' (p. 107).

This observation alone prevents us from treating his text as just history. Doing so will inevitably lead to our history becoming our destiny. These are the findings of a courageous, upright, and patriotic warrior. They demand, for our own survival, our closest attention.

Notes

1. General Agha Mohammad Yahya Khan, *The Breaking of Pakistan*, Islamabad: Al Basit, 1972.
2. Lieutenant General A.A.K. Niazi, *The Betrayal of East Pakistan*, Karachi: Oxford University Press, 1998.
3. Major General Rao Farman Ali, *How Pakistan Got Divided*, Lahore: Jang Publishers, 1992; Kamal Matinuddin, *Tragedy of Error 1968–1971*, Lahore: Wajid Alis, 1994; Major General Hakeem Arshad Qureshi, *The 1971 Indo-Pakistan War: A Soldier's Narrative*, Karachi: Oxford University Press, 2002; Major General A.O. Mitha, *Unlikely Beginnings: A Soldier's Life*, Karachi, Oxford University Press, 2003.
4. Brigadier Siddiq Salik, *Witness to Surrender*, Karachi: Oxford University Press, 1977; Brigadier A.R. Siddiqi, *East Pakistan: The End Game*, Karachi: Oxford University Press, 2004.

5. The report was prepared by a commission appointed by Bhutto in 1972 and led by Chief Justice Hamoodur Rahman. Rahman was a Bengali but chose to remain in Pakistan. The report was withheld by the Government of Pakistan. A purported text of the report was published in *India Today*, in December 2000. Then, what is said to be the complete text, was released by the Government of Pakistan, although there is speculation that some secret documents had been withheld. The text was published as *The Report of the Hamoodur Rahman Commission of Inquiry into the 1971 War as Declassified by the Government of Pakistan* (Lahore: Vanguard, 2001). The report is highly critical of the military leadership for strategic and tactical errors and misjudgements and for its treatment of the Bengali population. It also criticizes Bhutto's concept of two majorities in Pakistan: that of the PPP in West Pakistan and of the Awami League in East Pakistan. The commission states that Bhutto's concept might be fit for a confederalist system, not a federalist one. It also notes that the Awami League held a majority in the assembly with the power to impose a constitution for Pakistan. The commission suggested that Yahya and his associates, such as Tikka Khan, should be tried for illegal usurpation of power from Ayub Khan, but no trials were held.

6. The Tashkent Declaration was signed by President Ayub Khan for Pakistan and Prime Minister Lal Bahadur Shastri for India on 10 January 1966 in the capital of Uzbekistan where the two leaders had been invited by Aleksei Kosygin, the Soviet Prime Minister. Kosygin acted as a mediator between the two states. Ayub was opposed by the then Foreign Minister, Zulfikar Ali Bhutto. Despite Bhutto's opposition, Ayub joined Shastri in signing the document. The two countries agreed to withdraw their troops to the boundaries existing before the 1965 conflict. The usual clause to work toward the peaceful settlement of their disputes was agreed to, a clause that has had no positive effect.

7. The Six Points were announced in Lahore in November 1966 by Sheikh Mujibur Rahman and formed the basis of the manifesto of the Awami League in the 1970 election. These points were: (1) a federal parliamentary government with free and regular elections; (2) federal government to control foreign affairs and defence; (3) a separate currency or separate fiscal accounts for each province to control movement of capital from east to west; (4) all power of taxation at the provincial level with the federal government subsisting on grants from the provinces; (5) each federating unit could enter foreign trade agreements on its own and control the foreign exchange earned; (6) each unit could raise its own militia.

8. In 1947 Pakistan consisted of two wings—East and West. In 1955, all the provinces and states in West Pakistan were merged into a single administrative entity under the One Unit Scheme by President Ayub Khan. This was done to facilitate the process of constitution making, to ensure the basis of parity between the two wings of the country and to promote national integration by

erasing provincial boundaries. The One Unit system was dissolved on 1 July 1970 and all the provinces were restored.

9. The Legal Framework Order issued on 31 March 1970, contained the following points: (1) Pakistan must be based on Islamic ideology; (2) the country must have a democratic Constitution providing free and fair elections; (3) Pakistan's territory must be upheld in the Constitution; (4) the disparity between the wings, particularly in economic development, must be eliminated by statutory provisions to be guaranteed by the Constitution; (5) the distribution of power must be made in such a way that the provinces enjoy the maximum of autonomy consistent with giving the Central Government sufficient power to discharge its federal responsibilities, including the maintenance of the country's territorial integrity.

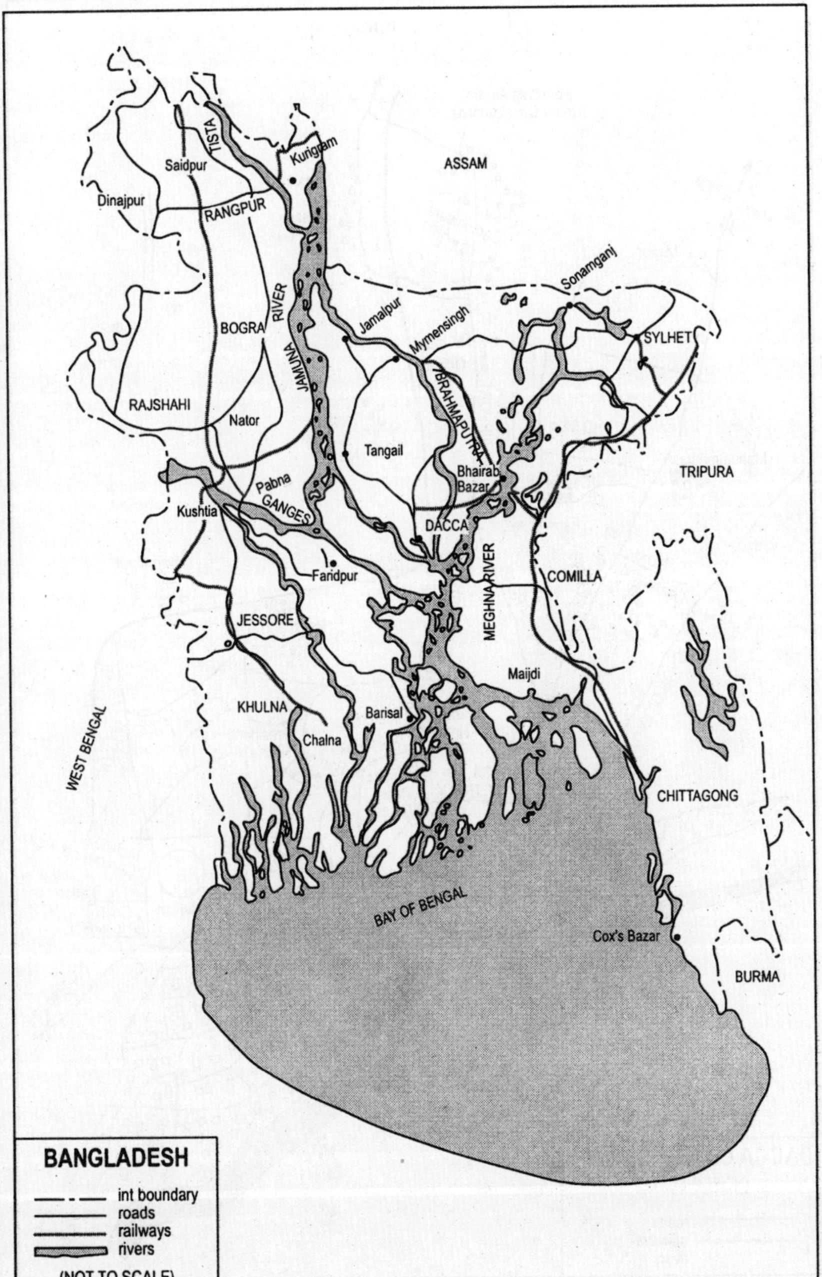
ASSAM
Kurigram
TISTA
Saidpur
Dinajpur
RANGPUR
Sonamganj
SYLHET
Jamalpur
Mymensingh
BOGRA
RIVER
JAMUNA
BRAHMAPUTRA
RAJSHAHI
Nator
Tangail
Bhairab Bazar
TRIPURA
Pabna
GANGES
Kushtia
DACCA
MEGHNA RIVER
Faridpur
COMILLA
JESSORE
Maijdi
KHULNA
Barisal
Chalna
WEST BENGAL
CHITTAGONG
BAY OF BENGAL
Cox's Bazar
BURMA
BANGLADESH
int boundary
roads
railways
rivers
(NOT TO SCALE)

DACCA CITY and CANTT
(NOT TO SCALE)

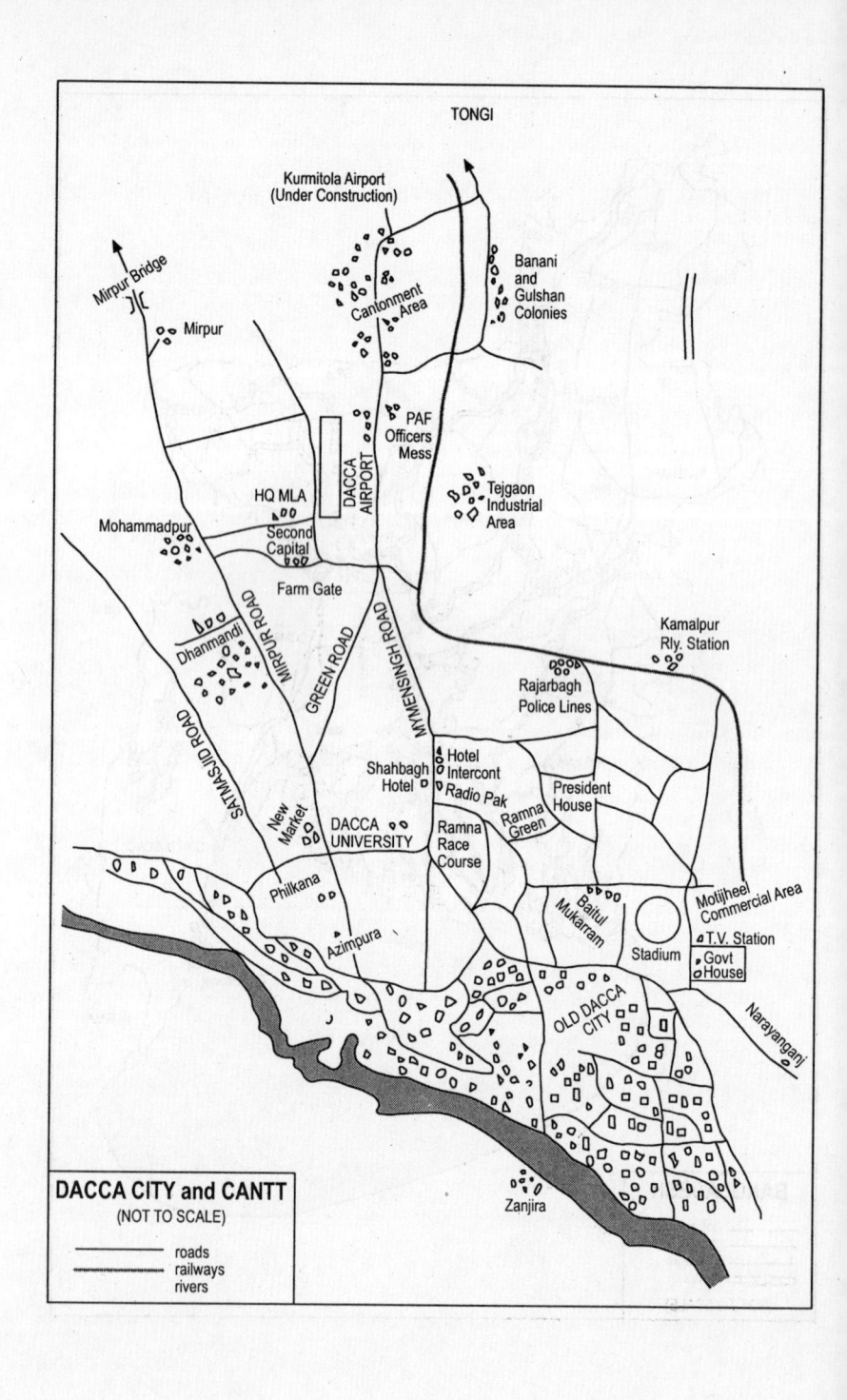

— roads
═ railways
  rivers

Locations shown on map:

- TONGI
- Kurmitola Airport (Under Construction)
- Mirpur Bridge
- Mirpur
- Cantonment Area
- Banani and Gulshan Colonies
- PAF Officers Mess
- HQ MLA
- DACCA AIRPORT
- Mohammadpur
- Second Capital
- Tejgaon Industrial Area
- Farm Gate
- Dhanmandi
- MIRPUR ROAD
- GREEN ROAD
- MYMENSINGH ROAD
- Kamalpur Rly. Station
- SATMASJID ROAD
- Rajarbagh Police Lines
- New Market
- Shahbagh Hotel
- Hotel Intercont
- Radio Pak
- President House
- DACCA UNIVERSITY
- Ramna Race Course
- Ramna Green
- Philkana
- Azimpura
- Baitul Mukarram
- Stadium
- Motijheel Commercial Area
- T.V. Station
- Govt House
- OLD DACCA CITY
- Narayanganj
- Zanjira

1

The Brewing Storm

Late in 1967, General Headquarters detailed me to attend the Army War Course beginning in February 1968. The course had been held at the army's Command and Staff College in Quetta for the preceding few years. It was meant to train senior army officers in the higher direction of war and staff duties at that level. The course also had one representative each from the navy and air force. In the first few years of its existence, the course had developed a poor reputation. Officers who could not be accommodated in appropriate jobs were detailed for this course. Consequently, it had acquired the droll subtitle of 'pre-retirement' training. With a few honourable exceptions, no one taking the course was promoted to higher positions of responsibility. To remedy this situation, the Chief of the General Staff personally selected officers for the 1968 War Course. This appeared to have worked, as more than half of us reached the rank of 'General'. The War Course turned out to be an interesting experience, despite the fact that I was initially disgruntled at being chosen for it.

In early 1966, when Headquarters 4 Corps was raised at Multan, the new Corps Commander, Lieutenant General M. Attiqur Rahman, selected me as his Chief of Staff. It was a challenge for all of us on the staff because the sister corps

HQ, 1 Corps, had been established quite a few years earlier. However, we galvanized ourselves into an effective team and devoted all our energies to the task at hand. By the end of 1966, we were able to deploy ourselves in the field and exercise effective command and control over all the formations under our command. We practised various operations of war with the same dexterity as any other formation at an equivalent level. In fact, we were quite proud of ourselves. In the subsequent months, during 1967, the Corps Commander tested us thoroughly and concluded that his formation was fully trained and ready for war. For this level of training and readiness I, being his Chief of Staff, was given the credit. Perhaps this explains why I was not so thrilled at being selected for a course that was meant to teach me all that I had already learnt through experience. However, General Headquarters has a reputation for making decisions which are difficult to understand; hence, I packed my bags and went to Quetta in early 1968.

As mentioned earlier, the War Course turned out to be an interesting experience. In fact, it was a paid holiday for professional self-study. We were a group of selected officers with professional interests, and the directing staff was there to guide our studies within the prescribed subjects and syllabi. We were required to conduct individual studies, spread over the entire course, on assigned subjects, in addition to having to study a great deal as preparation for our individual and collective assignments. My study on the training and utilization of manpower in Pakistan was forwarded to the Government of Pakistan by General Headquarters. In those days, President Ayub Khan had appointed a commission to study the subject and recommend a national policy. As a collective effort, the course produced a study on the 'Defence of Pakistan'. This study was also sent to levels higher than the Staff College and appreciated there. As a senior student, I had guided the course discussions on various topics. I had appointed Brigadier Mohammad Asghar (later Member of the National Assembly and Political Adviser to the President) as the secretary to coordinate this work, and he did an admirable job.

In October 1968, participants of the Army War Course visited the Rawalpindi area as part of a study tour. The course was granted an hour-long audience with the then-President, Field Marshal Mohammad Ayub Khan. We were informed that most of the audience was to be spent in questions and answers. As a senior student, I had coordinated various questions that were to be asked of the President. The President had just recovered from a serious and prolonged illness, details of which had been kept under wraps. He was now back in the saddle and working regularly. Though he looked a little weary, he was still beaming with confidence and apparently working hard and at peak efficiency. He casually mentioned that he had risen at four o'clock that morning to work on an important speech which he was scheduled to deliver in the near future. He answered all our questions with a great deal of aplomb. When it was my turn to present the last question, I asked him if we were following the British custom of having a shadow cabinet from the opposition. The President appeared to be visibly worked up and said that the opposition in Pakistan was of little consequence and had no following. Instead of giving a straight answer, he posed a counter question by asking, 'Which buffoon do I talk to?'

Although, as career army officers, we had a set of duties to perform that kept us busy, the political landscape of the nation was beginning to see a change. Seeds of political unrest and agitation were being sown as Zulfikar Ali Bhutto was mustering up the courage to speak against the President's policies. He was assisted by Dr Mahbub ul Haq's slogan of 'twenty-two families', according to which the rich were growing richer and the poor were becoming poorer. They vocalized the socialist slogan that there must be an equitable distribution of wealth. Besides the economic issues, Bhutto also started propagating that the Tashkent Agreement was a 'sell out' by the Government of Pakistan. He threatened to expose all the ugly details before the nation, at an appropriate time. This fired the imagination of the man on the street and the students. Thus, President Ayub Khan was politically checkmated. By clever political manoeuvring and manipulation, Bhutto was able to raise an army of agitators who were at his beck and call. He projected himself as the champion of the masses and raised the slogan of '*roti, kapra aur makan*'.*

Meanwhile, retired Air Marshal Asghar Khan also began to raise his voice in opposition to President Ayub Khan. He stated his views in the 'Letters to the Editor' section of the daily press, which brought him to the fore in the agitation against the government. He formed his own political party, Tehrik-e-Istiqlal. Bhutto made clever use of this situation, without granting any concessions or entering into any formal alliance with Asghar Khan. Eventually, Bhutto reaped a full political harvest at the expense of Asghar Khan. At least, that is how the political observers saw it then and later.

---

* Food, clothing, and housing.

At about this time (November 1968), two incidents took place separately and independently of each other: A student agitator of the Rawalpindi Polytechnic was killed by the police[1] and another agitator unsuccessfully shot at President Ayub Khan,[2] while he was addressing a public meeting in Peshawar. Despite the occurence of these two incidents, which considerably intensified political tension in West Pakistan, it was the government's raising of the price of sugar by 50 paisas per kilogram that proved to be the final straw. Anti-government riots broke out in Rawalpindi and Lahore and spread like wildfire to the other major cities of West Pakistan.

In the meantime, the participants of the Army War Course moved to Dhaka to see and study the defence problems of East Pakistan. Our stay in East Pakistan lasted fifteen days. Governor Abdul Monem Khan granted us an audience, during which he claimed the credit for peace and tranquillity in the province. It is hard to believe that he could not read the signs of brewing trouble. West Pakistan was already stricken with widespread anti-government riots, and East Pakistan was just waiting for a spark to set it ablaze. The spark was not long in coming, and within a short time the situation got out of control in both the wings.

Soon after our arrival in Dhaka, I was taken aback by the chasm that was apparent between the two wings of a united Pakistan. The Bengalis in East Pakistan were openly critical of the West Pakistanis in general and of the Punjabis, in particular. The majority of Bengalis held the Biharis in equal contempt. They were looked upon as foreign usurpers who had forged ahead of the locals in every competitive field of human endeavour. We were told that while referring to West

Pakistanis and the immigrants from Bihar, who had arrived post-partition, the average Bengali used derogatory words like '*shala** Punjabi' and '*shala* Bihari'. The reaction against Urdu was so strong that only Bengali language signboards were allowed to be displayed in East Pakistan. Signboards in both Urdu and English were either taken down or destroyed. Throughout the province, there was an atmosphere of tension which reflected the unhappiness of the average Bengali with the West Pakistanis. This anti-West Pakistan feeling was evinced even by the Bengali shopkeepers who would pay scant attention to a West Pakistani customer. They were not even interested in earning money from West Pakistani customers. In fact, they deliberately ignored and slighted them, and gave preference to Bengali customers. The environment was so strikingly unfriendly that I felt like a stranger in my own country, and totally unwelcome as a West Pakistani. Barely two weeks after we departed from East Pakistan, anti-government riots broke out in full force. The evident complacency of the Governor left us totally bewildered.

Like all good things, the Army War Course came to an end after ten months in December 1968. In the middle of 1968, Major General Mohammad Shariff (later Chairman, Joint Chiefs of Staff) had taken over as Commandant of the Staff College. He took a keen interest in the War Course and devoted a lot of time to it. On completion of the course, in addition to the traditional closing address, he interviewed all the students individually. He congratulated me on my exceptional performance and offered me the opportunity to stay on as the Chief Instructor in place of Brigadier

---

* A pejorative term which literally means brother-in-law, but is used as an abuse.

Mohammad Rahim Khan (later Major General), who had completed his tenure and was due for a posting. However, I wanted a different posting because of my already prolonged experience at the Staff College in both the Tactical (1952–55) and Staff Wings (1958–61). My request was granted and I was posted as Commander of the Artillery 2 Corps with headquarters at Lahore.

At this juncture, I would like to narrate a small incident which proved to be of great significance and gave a lead to future events. During the month of January 1969, I visited General Headquarters in connection with the raising of Headquarters Artillery 2 Corps. While in Rawalpindi, I made an appointment for an evening social call on Lieutenant General Gul Hassan at his residence. He had recently taken over as Chief of the General Staff. His predecessor, Major General Yaqub Khan, had vast experience of commanding the Armoured Division, the Command and General Staff College. He had also been Chief of General Staff for quite some time. All of a sudden, he was bundled off as a student on the Imperial Defence College course. This clumsy and unceremonious action was obviously taken to get him out of the way.

Lieutenant General Gul Hassan was elated at this powerful new post and at the patronage of his Chief, General Yahya Khan. During my evening call, our conversation revolved around topical subjects like the prevailing unrest and the law and order situation in the country. Gul Hassan openly criticized Field Marshal Ayub Khan's sons who, according to him, were letting their father down by amassing wealth by unfair means. At one point, Gul Hassan became quite animated and 'blurted' out that 'I have told the old cock that this time we will impose Martial Law and take control ourselves but not protect Ayub and his henchmen.' The reference was to General Yahya Khan, Commander-in-Chief of the Pakistan army.

I had taken two months overseas leave for Haj. On 2 February 1969, we (my wife Rafia and I) proceeded to Saudi Arabia. During Hajj, I had the opportunity to meet Muslims from several countries, ranging from the Maghreb* to the Philippines and, in particular, Muslims from India. Each one of them was distressed at the agitation and rioting against the Ayub government. They invariably opined that the Pakistani nation was committing a grave error and would regret this emotional flare-up in the years to come. They also expressed the view that Ayub Khan had built up an image of Pakistan as a strong and prosperous country that was a force to reckon with. The Indian Muslims were particularly distressed since Pakistan's strength as a country, and its leadership, were, by proxy, a source of pride and reassurance for them in their unenviable predicament as a victimized minority in a predominantly Hindu India. After the end of our Hajj, we went to Baghdad, where we heard the news of President Ayub Khan's resignation (25 March 1969). After Ayub's departure, General Yahya Khan assumed power and proclaimed himself both the President and Chief Martial Law Administrator.

On my return from Haj, I called on Headquarters Martial Law Zone 'B' (West Pakistan). This was my old Headquarters 4 Corps, which I had helped to raise. It was whispered to me, by a senior staff officer, that Martial Law instructions initially

---

* The western region of North Africa, including the five modern countries of Morocco with Western Sahara, Algeria, Tunisia, Libya, and Mauritania.

issued by General Headquarters were in support of the Ayub government, but were immediately withdrawn. General Yahya Khan was persuaded to change his mind and insisted on President Ayub Khan's resignation. I checked this story with Lieutenant General M. Attiqur Rahman who categorically denied it and told me that he had received only one set of orders which were implemented, wherein General Yahya Khan was proclaimed as the Chief Martial Law Administrator.

At the end of my leave, I returned to the job of raising Headquarters Artillery 2 Corps at Lahore. Not long afterwards, however, I received orders to move over and assume command of 107 Brigade. This was sudden, as I was in the midst of inspecting one of my units at Jhelum when the news was flashed to me. In fact, no one around me, myself included, knew the location of 107 Brigade. Later that day, I went to Headquarters 1 Corps at Mangla where the Corps Commander Lieutenant General Tikka Khan confided that I had been approved for promotion. I was to move to Jessore in East Pakistan, get some experience of that province, and then take charge of the Division at Dhaka from Major General Muzaffaruddin.

I lost no time in packing my bags and making yet another move to a distant station, as only three months earlier I had been posted to Lahore. Without even a briefing at Dhaka, I made my way to Jessore and took over command of the 107 Brigade where, in addition, I was to be the Sub-Administrator of Martial Law of Khulna Division. Apart from the routine Martial Law work, my duties included the task of maintaining law and order in my area of responsibility.

Jessore's location posed a peculiar problem. It had a very long border, not based on any natural features or obstacles, with Indian Bengal, resulting in virtually free movement across the border. Calcutta (now Kolkata), the capital of Indian West Bengal, was only forty miles away. Besides, there was a 20 per cent Hindu minority on Pakistani territory. This provided ideal conditions for infiltration, subversion, and sabotage from, and for, a hostile India. There was also a big labour force in Khulna which was seething with unrest. They were exposed to bribes and subversion by a potent Hindu minority, the underground Communist element, and the Awami League militants who were receiving all kinds of support and sympathy from across the border.

There were no major outbreaks of violence during the three months I was in Jessore, but the situation was explosive and pregnant with portents of the disaster which was to follow. Local Muslim League leaders, like Abdus Sabur Khan, were lying low whereas Sheikh Mujibur Rahman openly toured the area and delivered fiery speeches to local gatherings, in flagrant violation of Martial Law orders. He played upon the Bengalis' sense of deprivation and blamed their woes on the Central Government, and the '*shala* Punjabis' and '*shala* Biharis', who were the patent objects of his vicious attacks. He was declared a sacred cow by the Chief Martial Law Administrator and we could not touch him. Taking advantage of this undeclared amnesty, Mujib, who addressed massive crowds at his meetings, lashed out mercilessly at the Central Government and succeeded in spreading hatred against all non-Bengalis. Even the soldiers openly participated in his political meetings and fell prey to his propaganda, hook, line and sinker.

Meanwhile, the Bengali officers in the formation had withdrawn into a shell of their own and rarely mixed with their West Pakistani brethren. Their families also kept aloof. Every evening, they would get together in small groups among themselves. Since these were purely Bengali gatherings, it was not possible to penetrate them and get to know what was going on. Genuinely sincere and friendly advances by the Brigade Commander and his family elicited no response from the Bengali officers. The 1 East Bengal Regiment, commanded by Lieutenant Colonel Golam Dastagir, remained the hub of Bengali activity. In a minor incident, Golam Dastagir exchanged some hot words with the Commanding Officer of the 27 Baluch Regiment, who was a Christian from Lahore. Though the details may be unimportant, the incident, nonetheless, reflected the poison that had permeated the minds of the Bengalis and had laid a strong foundation of anti-West Pakistan sentiment, even among the elite and well-disciplined class of senior army officers.

I noted, with special regret, that no non-Awami League leader could muster enough guts or command a sufficient following to hold a public meeting and talk of national unity and one Pakistan. There was no public figure to repudiate all the falsehood that Sheikh Mujib was propagating. Sheikh Mujib was quoting patently false statistics and figures on how East Pakistan was earning all the foreign exchange that was being spent on the development of West Pakistan. There was never a rebuttal to this from any organ of the Central Government either. Results of development projects undertaken during the Ayub regime were all too visible while travelling around East Pakistan, but not a word was said or written about this irrefutable evidence. Bengalis, in general, were dreaming of a

'*Sonar Bangla*',* which was expected to be a 'heaven on earth'. At that time they had lost all sense of reality for they did not realize that, on its own, their land had nothing much to offer other than hunger and poverty for the masses. With few natural resources and an exploding population, it was not hard to see the shape of things to come. However, when emotions overpower reason, people lose all sense of balance and plunge into certain disaster without caring to look over their shoulders.

Notes

1. 7 November 1968: A college student, Abdul Hamid, was shot dead when police opened fire on a procession of students demonstrating on Peshawar Road, Rawalpindi. The students were demonstrating against the new education policy summarized in the University Ordinance.
2. 11 November 1968: A young man named Hashim attempted to assassinate President Ayub Khan at a meeting arranged by the Muslim League in Peshawar.

---

* Golden Bengal.

2

Prelude to the 1970 Elections

In mid-October 1969, I moved to Dhaka to replace Major General Muzaffaruddin and to assume greater responsibility, covering the entire province of East Pakistan. I spent a few days with him before he departed for West Pakistan. I was curious to learn about the Agartala Conspiracy Case,[1] as I had only read about it in the press. Muzaffaruddin told me, in all earnestness, that the case was based on reality. Sheikh Mujibur Rahman was genuinely implicated. Some Bengali troops were to launch surprise attacks at night and capture quarter guards and armouries of the West Pakistani military units. These units would be disarmed and confined to the barracks as prisoners of war. This success was expected to induce the remaining Bengali troops to join forces with the rebels. The Government of East Pakistan would automatically fall, and rebels would take control. The Government of India was to assist in various ways, such as banning over-flights from West Pakistan. However, the government's prosecution team, comprising mostly of retired judges, was in no hurry to complete the case. They let it drag on until subsequent events overtook it, and eventually President Ayub Khan was forced to withdraw the case, release Sheikh Mujib, and enter into fruitless negotiations with the agitators, which lasted till he was toppled.

The day I arrived in Dhaka to succeed Major General Muzaffaruddin, I found out that Major General Ghulam Umar, then Chief of National Security and very close to President Yahya Khan, was staying next door. As he was departing for Rawalpindi the same evening, I took the opportunity to exchange views with him because I was quite perturbed about what I had seen during the last three months.

While discussing the situation in East Pakistan, I told Umar categorically that in my assessment Sheikh Mujib would 'sweep the board', to the extent of 75 per cent, in East Pakistan. The Central Government had already announced that elections would be held before the end of 1970. This gave the Awami League leadership more than a year to play upon the sense of deprivation already felt, rightly or wrongly, by the average East Pakistani. I emphasized that if the Chief Martial Law Administrator seriously wanted to hand over power to the winner after the elections, he should be prepared to entrust it to Sheikh Mujib, in spite of his Six Points; also, that there were several elements in West Pakistan who would be very willing to cooperate with him and join his government. I further emphasized that having conducted a 'fair' election under the guard of Martial Law bayonets, the President would have no excuse whatsoever for not handing over power to the majority party. Major General Ghulam Umar was also told that Sheikh Mujib never talked of one Pakistan, so he would inevitably continue to dwell on the deprivation of the Bengalis. He was propagating an independent sovereign state of Bangla Desh, which he referred to as *Sonar Bangla*, which would be a land of plenty with prosperity for all its inhabitants. He repeatedly quoted fictitious figures supplied by the Bengali staff at the Planning Commission, which the Central Government, at any level, did not bother to refute.

All the propaganda by Sheikh Mujib and his party added fuel to the fire of hatred against the *shala* Punjabis' who symbolized the 'colonialism' of the Central Government. I felt that we were playing into the hands of the secessionists. They were bound to win the elections on their platform, and the Chief Martial Law Administrator would then be forced to bow down to the pressure and demands of the majority party. Major General Ghulam Umar appeared incredulous because not only was my statement in contrast, notably, to his own assessment, but also to the views of the agencies that reported to him. I am not sure whether I succeeded in making the desired impact because, in the months to follow, he never bothered to have another session with me. However, I do distinctly remember that after the elections, and the unhappy aftermath, when I reminded Umar of our conversation of October 1969, he conceded somewhat mournfully that I was unfortunately right but that there was very little anybody could have done to reverse the situation.

During my time in Jessore and later in Dhaka, but before the 1970 elections, Bengali sentiments against the West Pakistani troops were fanned to such a degree by the Awami League that it became impossible for soldiers to travel alone or even in groups of twos or threes. There were a few incidents where West Pakistani soldiers were severely beaten up by Bengali mobs on little or no pretext. Eventually, to protect their morale, troops were ordered to travel in bodies of not less than ten, under a non-commissioned officer. They were to carry personal arms with live ammunition and use these in self-defence. After this order was put into effect, there were no further incidents of this nature with the exception of one big incident in Chittagong. A large crowd of locals tried to mob a fairly large body of West Pakistani troops. Although the troops were carrying arms and ammunition, they only used their rifle butts to disperse the mob. An inquiry into the incident, to be conducted by the Commissioner of Chittagong Division, was ordered by the Governor, but it remained inconclusive like most such inquiries.

While we are on the early period of my posting at Dhaka, I would like to mention one specific incident which took place during the first fortnight and which aptly portrays the political situation in East Pakistan at that time. One day, while getting ready to attend a *meena bazaar** organized by the East Pakistan Rifles, for the benefit of the troops' families, I received a phone call from the Governor's House asking me to attend an urgent meeting about some minor riots that had erupted that afternoon. The riots were directed against the Bihari community, in particular, and the West Pakistanis, in general. As I proceeded to leave my house to attend the meeting, I could see that Dhaka was in flames; billowing clouds of smoke were visible all over the city. As a result of the meeting at the Governor's House, my troops were deployed in sensitive areas, in addition to the police and the East Pakistan Rifles.

The next day, Lieutenant General Sahibzada Yaqub Khan, Commander Eastern Command, decided to show the flag and take a ride around the riot-affected areas. We were shown how

---

* A fair organized by women for women.

the Bengali crowd had surged forward and attacked various Bihari areas, including the township of Mohammedpur. We also drove to the particular spot where Lieutenant Colonel Syed Akabar Hussain Shah, at great personal risk, had saved the lives of many Biharis. During the tour we received an urgent call from the Governor, asking us to attend yet another meeting that was to take place in the Durbar Hall, where all the prominent politicians and citizens of Dhaka were assembled. The Governor opened the meeting by saying that the purpose of the assembly was to form Joint Mohalla* Peace Committees, to rebuild confidence among the warring communities. After the Governor had finished, Mr Ataur Rahman, a former Chief Minister of East Pakistan and now considered an elder statesman, got up to speak on behalf of the gathered assembly. He said that he was speaking on behalf of the East Pakistani people who wanted to know when the 'West Pakistan Army of Occupation' would leave East Pakistan, to allow its people to determine their own future freely. This statement was made loudly and clearly, amidst pin-drop silence, but elicited not a single response from the full Durbar Hall. Ataur Rahman's statement came as a great shock and still rings in my ears. I will never forget the scene as long as I live. It clearly indicated the polarization that had taken place by then.

During the first day of rioting, two non-commissioned officers from my artillery, who looked obviously West Pakistani even out of uniform, were stabbed to death in the New Market Area. They had gone to attend the *meena bazaar* organized by the East Pakistan Rifles in Peel Khana. We traced the assassins to Awami League hooligans who, to

---
* Neighbourhood.

escape the law, had taken refuge in the Jagan Nath Hall, a student hostel of Dhaka University. The hostels were sacrosanct, even during the Martial Law. Later, one of the culprits was apprehended during the Operation Searchlight.

At this stage, it is important for the reader to know the army's command and control set-up at Dhaka. During the period of Major General Muzaffaruddin's command, all power and authority in the province was vested in him as he was the General Officer Commanding (GOC) 14 Division. By virtue of this appointment, he was the General Officer Commanding East Pakistan as well. Upon imposition of Martial Law, he was also appointed Martial Law Administrator Zone 'B', as well as Governor of East Pakistan. This structure was reconstituted on the departure of Major General Muzaffaruddin. Admiral Syed Mohammad Ahsan, Commander-in-Chief, Pakistan Navy, was appointed Governor. The military establishment was also reorganized. All static units, like the East Bengal Regimental Centre, the Combined Military Hospital, and the Ordnance Depot were organized into the East Pakistan Logistic Area and placed under the command of Brigadier (later Major General) Mohammad Hussain Ansari. The 14 Division, divested of all these static elements, was placed under my command, with the task of defending East Pakistan. A superior military headquarters, with the glorified title of the Eastern Command, was established under the command of Lieutenant General Yaqub Khan. In actual fact, this headquarters had only one infantry division and the logistical area under its command. It lacked the military resources of a proper corps headquarters. There should have been at least two more divisions, besides the complement of corps troops like armour, artillery, signals and engineers, and supporting services.

By virtue of my appointment, I was also the Deputy Martial Law Administrator. Major General Rao Farman Ali Khan, who was adviser to the Governor, also acted as a Liaison Officer between the Civil Government and the Martial Law authority. There was an inherent contradiction in this arrangement: whereas the Governor was the head of the civil administration, the Martial Law Administrator considered himself the supreme authority. To a great extent, it was due to the personal tact and understanding of these gentlemen, and the diplomacy displayed by Major General Farman, that disputes were avoided at the highest level. However, there was some visible friction, despite the fact that both the Governor and the Martial Law Administrator were cultured gentlemen, besides being personal friends. Farman's importance, as far as the two top office-holders were concerned, could be judged from the fact that when the President agreed to an immediate posting-out, and relief, of Major General Farman, both the Governor and the Martial Law Administrator intervened and persuaded the President to maintain the status quo and cancel his orders.

It would not be out of place to narrate an interesting little anecdote in connection with Farman's posting. In Dhaka city, there lived a Hindu jeweller known as Kala Chand who was known more for his knowledge of palmistry and fortune telling than for his skill at making ornaments. He had access to most military families, including mine. He claimed to have read the palms of all the previous GOCs in Dhaka, and showed a keenness to read my palm as well. One day, he managed to corner me and Brigadier Farman at my residence (his promotion to Major General came later). In my case, in reply to a specific question, he said that I would go back to

West Pakistan with respect and honour by June 1971. This was not difficult for me to guess because I was due to complete my tenure by June 1971. However, in the case of Farman, he predicted a long stay, even though Farman had already completed his tenure.

This was not the only encounter the two of us had with Kala Chand. The second one proved more prescient. After obtaining the President's agreement regarding his posting away from East Pakistan, Brigadier Farman accompanied me to my residence from the airport. Coincidently, we came across Kala Chand at the house. Farman decided to test Kala Chand. The palmist first read my palm. While he had nothing fresh to add, this time he stated that I would leave with respect and honour in April 1971. In the case of Brigadier Farman, however, Kala Chand again predicted a long stay. Farman chided him for being totally wrong, as the President had just issued orders for his move back to West Pakistan and he would be gone within a week. Kala Chand looked at his palm again, this time more carefully; he shook his head and said that this was not to be. He told Farman that, very soon, he would be promoted to the rank of a General, but that he had a long stay in East Pakistan all the same. This turned out to be amazingly accurate. Although I have never been an advocate of palmistry, this incident has left me in two minds about its accuracy.

To get back to our story, as the second-in-command and Deputy Martial Administrator, I used to assume nominal charge of the Martial Law administration whenever General Yaqub left the province. These absences were few, and never more than for a few days at a time. Almost invariably, the

Governor would also be away at these times as the Chief Martial Law Administrator's conferences required the participation of both. I confined myself to routine matters or any problems that needed immediate decisions, yet there were strains and stresses as law and order problems repeatedly cropped up in one place or another. For example, Maulana Bhashani once held a rally in Dhaka which passed peacefully although he had threatened '*gherao*'* and '*jalao*'†.

My brigade commanders and other officers of the Division were heavily engaged in Martial Law duties throughout the province. However, they remained committed to their primary functions of command and operational preparedness. In spite of inherent organizational flaws, we ran a tension-free team in the province. A lot of realistic training was carried out at all levels. Defence plans were tested and reviewed in every sector of the province. Officers ranked Major and above, from the entire Division, participated in the war games in each sector. All operational areas were thoroughly reconnoitred, and physical movement of troops and logistics were tested. All these preparations paid dividends later when the Division was found to be fully prepared for the events that followed.

During the period prior to the elections in 1970, we were regularly visited by the Director General of the Inter-Services Intelligence, Major General Mohammad Akbar Khan and the Director of the Intelligence Bureau (IB), Mr Rizvi. They maintained regular personal contact with me and exchanged views. However, they had their own respective staffs in East Pakistan, who were all Bengalis, with one notable exception.

---

* Surround.
† Burn.

This was Lieutenant Colonel Riaz Ahmed of the IB, whom I had known well for a long time. He was a dependable officer who rendered valuable advice to me, though he did not have to report to me. I have reason to believe that there was a lot of misreporting by these two agencies. Some of it may have been inadvertent, but a lot of it may have been deliberate in order to misguide the authorities. These advisers of the President appeared to believe that the vote in East Pakistan would be divided. According to them, it was not possible for the Awami League to win a decisive majority. They failed to see the obvious writing on the wall. Some of these gentlemen surreptitiously went about trying to reinvigorate political opposition to the Awami League through money and the moral support of the Central Government. These crude attempts leaked out and eventually produced negative results. There was a lot of resentment among the educated masses.

During all these months of 1969 and 1970, none of the principal staff officers of the General Headquarters visited East Pakistan. The only exception was Lieutenant General Gul Hassan, who came for a few days and paid a visit to Jessore during my tenure there. President Yahya Khan and General Abdul Hamid Khan (Chief of Army Staff) paid regular visits. In fact, the two were invariably together in East Pakistan, but never travelled by the same flight. On each visit, military officers of the rank of Colonel and above were required to be present at the airport on their arrival and departure. The Governor and the Martial Law Administrator accompanied them to the President's House, where they were left to their own pursuits. It was rumoured that disreputable women visited the President's House during Yahya Khan's trips to Dhaka. It was also said that 'comfort girls' from West

Pakistan were provided by some gentlemen who were consolidating their positions with the President. To my great distress, these rumours were confirmed by my Intelligence staff.

Yahya Khan, during his visits, never consulted me in private. Once, we had him over for dinner with the officers of the Dhaka garrison. As I led him across the lawn to the dining room, he turned around and asked me if, as the President of Pakistan, there was anything he could do for my command. I am not very poetic but I resorted to Mirza Ghalib's verse to describe the situation:

'mushkilen mujh per parin itni ke asaan ho gayi'*

This seemed to amuse him and he had a hearty laugh. Many months later, when adversity brought the top military leadership closer together, both Admiral Ahsan and General Yaqub Khan confided to me, separately, that they also rarely got the President's ear alone. They would, upon his arrival in East Pakistan, drive the President to his place of stay in Dhaka. They would meet him again only when it was time for him to return to West Pakistan, when they would pick him up and drive him to the airport. In the interim, he was left alone with his chosen coterie, to mix work with pleasure, during his stay in Dhaka. Some of the happenings in the President's House, as reported by my Intelligence staff, are too disgraceful to be put into print.

There was occasional talk of subversion among the Bengali troops. The basic plan of the Agartala conspirators was fairly

---
* I have faced so many difficulties that facing them has become easy.

well known among the officers' corps. Even during my short tenure at Jessore, the attitude of the Bengali officers had caused me concern. Therefore, I shared my apprehensions with the commanding officers of the West Pakistani units, and ordered them to keep half of their personal weapons and ammunition in the barracks with the troops, to guard against surprise attacks.

The suspect loyalty of the Bengali troops, particularly the pure Bengali battalions, agitated me. We spoke of one country and one nation, and yet we were raising a separate Bengali army. I failed to understand why the infantry, from both wings of the country, could not be integrated into mixed battalions. After all, Punjabis, Pathans, and other ethnic groups were serving together in various units without any administrative or ethnic problems. In other fighting arms, like the artillery, the engineers and the signals, the Bengalis were well integrated with the West Pakistani troops. I was strongly of the opinion that all ethnic and linguistic groups must serve together as one national army. The British had divided us for their own purposes. We, however, needed to galvanize ourselves into one nation; the armed forces, I felt, should be the ones to lead in that direction.

I thought out a plan to integrate 25 per cent of the Bengalis into the West Pakistan infantry battalions in the first phase. This was to begin with units stationed in East Pakistan. I went over to the General Headquarters in Rawalpindi and had the plan approved by the Chief of the General Staff. As a pilot project, three battalions from my own formation, belonging to different groups of infantry, were selected for the induction of the first group of 25 per cent Bengalis. These were 27 Punjab in Rajshahi, 27 Baluch in Jessore, and 19 Frontier Force in Dhaka. The 19 Frontier Force, under Lieutenant Colonel Syed Akbar Hussain Shah, which was stationed at Dhaka, was the first to complete induction. A formal parade was held in the city; General Yaqub Khan took the salute, after which the Bengali personnel were sent on pre-embarkation leave. They all returned to duty, and there was not a single case of over-staying the leave or desertion. The battalion left for Chittagong, *en route** to Sialkot. I was greatly pleased at the success of this experiment, which had been my brainchild.

After the initial success, I expected to raise some more integrated units. However, to my utter surprise and dismay, orders were received from General Headquarters to raise three more purely Bengali infantry battalions. These were 8, 9, and 10 East Bengal battalions. The last one was to be a National Service Unit comprised of university students. To plead my case against this planned step, I sent Lieutenant Colonel Riaz Ahmed of the IB to Rawalpindi as I could not leave East Pakistan. He was a reliable officer, well-known to me personally, and to Lieutenant General Gul Hassan as well. He conveyed my message, describing the inherent dangers of this step. An already difficult situation was likely to become untenable, as it would result in a significant addition to the strength of the potential rebels. He returned empty-handed: the die had been cast and the decision could no longer be reversed. Consequently, the Commander, Logistic Area, was told to begin raising these new battalions. Without consulting me, the Quartermaster General at General Headquarters requisitioned their accommodations and decided on the

---

* A French phrase which means 'on the way'.

stations from which these battalions were to be raised. Much to my discomfiture, the 10 East Bengal Battalion was housed next door to my headquarters.

Shortly after these new 'raisings' were 'on the ground', we were visited by the Chief of Army Staff, General Abdul Hamid Khan. He chose Rangpur and Saidpur for his visit, and I naturally accompanied him. After his visit to Saidpur, we were to be picked up at Thakurgaon in North Bengal by a special plane. This was about one hour's drive from Saidpur. He took the steering wheel of the jeep himself and invited me to sit beside him. For the next one hour, we were alone while the entourage followed us. I used this opportunity for a heart to heart talk. In the first instance, I wanted to know why the successful induction of Bengalis into the infantry units had been abandoned. He told me that Lieutenant General Khwaja Wasiuddin, Master General of Ordnance at General Headquarters, Colonel Commandant of the East Bengal Regiment, and senior Bengali officers had exerted pressure for this step. Lieutenant General Wasiuddin had made it known that he was under such great pressure from senior Bengali officers in the army, who were agitating for this step, that he had suffered a heart attack; he pleaded that he could not resist them any longer. Therefore, General Headquarters decided to revert to the status quo and to raise purely Bengali battalions once more, to placate these dissenting Bengali officers.

I then suggested that the number of troops in East Pakistan was totally inadequate for the task assigned to us. This had become very evident during the 1965 War, when the feeling of isolation had overpowered not only the general populace but even the garrison. This was evident from the records pertaining to that period. General Hamid assured me that, in case of an emergency, General Headquarters had already drawn up plans to reinforce East Pakistan. I argued that as India would ban over-flights and would dominate the sea route, no reinforcements would be possible. Troops on the ground, however, would have a lot of deterrence value, compared to plans on paper. General Hamid did not have a convincing answer, and therefore parried the question. I had prepared a paper on this subject for Lieutenant General Yaqub Khan, but General Headquarters would not go back to the Induction Plan and we were forced to go ahead with the new raisings as ordered. The only concession granted to us was that the 57 Brigade group, under the command of the Command Brigadier (later Lieutenant General) Jahanzeb Arbab, arrived in Dhaka equipped with a full component of arms and services. We decided to house them in Dhaka. We also acquired three helicopters commanded by Lieutenant Colonel (later Major General) Naseerullah Khan Babar. Two of these were Alouettes, with a limited capacity, but the third was a Russian-built MI8 which could carry thirty fully armed troops.

Note

1. In the Agartala Conspiracy Case, thirty-five individuals, including Mujibur Rahman, were accused of 'plotting to deprive Pakistan of its sovereignty over a part of its territory by an armed revolt with weapons, ammunitions and funds provided by India.' It was alleged by the Pakistan government, in an announcement on 2 January 1968, that the plot was hatched in Agartala, the capital of the Indian state Tripura. It was suspected that an officer of the Indian High Commission in Dhaka was involved. The trial was never completed as the charges were dropped when Ayub resigned the presidency and Martial Law was imposed by Yahya Khan.

3

The Rising Sun of the Awami League

Late in 1969, the general elections' schedule was announced: elections would be held at the end of 1970. This gave the politicians more than one year for canvassing. In other words, too much time was being allowed for the generation of political 'heat', for the creation of polarization, and for tremendous strains to be created in the already charged atmosphere. In East Pakistan, the Awami League acquired all the time to think, plan, and execute its election strategy. Sheikh Mujib toured the province extensively, preaching his Six Points, which bordered on a demand for independence. With the passage of time, Mujib's stance became extremely militant and he was uncompromising in his demands. He talked more and more of *Sonar Bangla*—an independent East Bengal which would be a land of plenty and prosperity for everyone.

The Awami League organized its hooligan elements into an effective weapon. Their task was to intimidate and subdue their opponents, to prevent them from raising their voices. If the opposition dared to hold public meetings, these hooligan elements immediately went into action and disrupted the meetings. Important Muslim League leaders, like Nurul Amin, Abdus Sabur Khan, Fazlul Qader Chaudhry, and Maulvi Farid Ahmed could not hold and address political meetings. Once, Professor Ghulam Azam attempted to hold a meeting in defiance of these elements in Dhaka, but the Awami League ruffians broke up the meeting while the police remained idle spectators.

Maulana Bhashani was the only other leader who could still attract large crowds. Not very active, he mostly travelled around the countryside, nor did he confront Sheikh Mujib directly. He held only one rally in Dhaka, at the Paltan Maidan, during the whole of 1970. Although this meeting was quite successful and was executed without any interruption, the Maulana never repeated it.

Political meetings were held throughout the summer of 1970, and various intelligence agencies of the government kept reporting on them. Several times, President Yahya was annoyed about the contents of Sheikh Mujib's speeches and summoned him to explain his conduct. I was told, on very reliable authority, that on such occasions Sheikh Mujib was incredibly meek and apologetic and so, each time, successfully managed to dupe the President. He used the plea that everything he said on stage was for public consumption and appeasement; in reality, after the elections, he would do the President's bidding and follow his directions. I understand that he made many promises to General Yahya Khan that he never intended to keep.

The President's blind trust in Sheikh Mujib's promises caused a great deal of frustration among some intelligence agencies. One of them laid a trap for Sheikh Mujib. A recording device was planted in a car in which Sheikh Mujib, along with a confidant, was travelling. On the way, the confidant engaged

Sheikh Mujib in conversation. Unwittingly, Sheikh Mujib blurted out his real intentions[1]—he did not mean to keep any of his promises, and would show his real teeth once he had obtained a clear majority in the elections. I believe this tape was played for the President. He heard the truth in disbelief but did not move a muscle nor did he take any apparent action against Sheikh Mujib. It could be said that General Yahya Khan was overconfident about his own position, and felt that, by virtue of being the Chief Martial Law Administrator, he had unlimited powers which would enable him to outwit and outmanoeuvre his potential opponents. Later events proved how wrong he was.

A lot of preparatory work was done, by the civil government, to hold the elections on schedule. As the time drew nearer, the Awami League stepped up its campaign. Their dominance became more apparent, even to a layman, but the intelligence agencies stuck to their earlier predictions. Headquarters 14 Division was required to send regular monthly Intelligence summaries to higher headquarters, including General Headquarters and the headquarters of the Chief Martial Law Administrator. We kept reporting accurately and truthfully: by our reckoning, the Awami League would capture a minimum of 75 per cent of the National Assembly seats from East Pakistan. It appears that ours was a cry in the wilderness because the President's advisers stuck to their earlier estimates and fed him information accordingly.

While preparatory work for the elections was going on, President Yahya took some arbitrary and extraordinary steps which had profound political repercussions on the course of the country's future. Advised by Professor G.W. Choudhury of East Pakistan, he promulgated a Legal Framework Order under which the elections were to be held.[2] The salient points of this order were: (a) The province of West Pakistan was to be divided into the original four provinces; (b) The elections would be held under the principle of universal suffrage, i.e. one man, one vote.

The two points ensured a majority for East Pakistan, in terms of National Assembly seats, and hence a majority-say in the political decision-making process of the country. Thus the long-standing principle of parity between the country's two wings, which had been established by the political representatives of the two wings, was abolished arbitrarily. Though it is a matter of conjecture, it is reasonable to assume that this must have, in some ways, affected the political leadership of West Pakistan.

Life in West Pakistan was reported to be fairly normal. 'Politicking' did generate some heat, but not enough to disturb the social patterns of life. Club life and coffee parties went on as usual. Ambitious bureaucrats and service officers were busy discovering various means to get close to the President. We, in East Pakistan, on the other hand, seemed to move from one crisis to the next, and no one in the Western wing seemed to care. Before I 'bellyache' too much, I must confess that we also had our share of entertainment. I was able to get away, twice, to the tea gardens in Sylhet where I quenched my thirst for hunting. We also had our share of VVIP guests, including the King of Nepal, the Shahinshah of Iran, Reza Shah Pahlavi, and Prince Karim Aga Khan. Reza Shah Pahlavi, in response to our welcoming reception for him, treated us to a return banquet. At the banquet, except for the venue, everything was Iranian—the food, the flowers, the décor, and the serving staff had all been especially brought from Iran. The royal dancing troupe delighted us with a thrilling performance. The Shahinshah knew how to entertain in a befitting style!

In the weeks before the elections, the Governor called a conference which I attended along with General Yaqub Khan. He emphasized the President's objective that the elections should be totally fair and free. Troops would not be present at any polling station. The management of the polling stations was left in the hands of the Election Commission and the police. Troops would be stationed at a sufficient distance, but within striking distance of the polling, particularly in localities where trouble was anticipated. I have reason to believe that the President had been convinced by his advisers that the vote in East Pakistan would be split and, therefore, inconclusive. As a result, the contending political parties would have to look to him for support in forming the government at the centre. It appears that the President was misled. Some of the advice may have been inadvertently wrong, but in some cases the falsehoods were deliberate. I have reason to believe that the security adviser to the President was taken for a ride by his underlings who, in most cases, were local officers with parochial interests. The agencies that fed him information always reported on events that had already occurred, but said little about what was to come. Therefore, those in command were always left trailing the actual flow of events.

As the time for elections approached, political activity gained in tempo and momentum. Mujib and his party leaders launched a vicious campaign against the Central Government, which was alleged to be Punjabi-dominated. There was no hesitation in fabricating lies on all fronts. Unfortunately, the Central Government did not react and rebut any of the falsehoods that the people of East Pakistan swallowed in total innocence. Awami League ruffians used to break up any political meeting that the Opposition parties attempted to organize. Even intellectuals like Professor Rehman Sobhan and Dr Kamal Hossain led the chorus in fabricating lies about the economic figures and exaggerating the economic deprivation of the East Pakistanis, particularly the Bengalis of that province. Gradually, the Opposition parties were swept off the board and the Awami League began to dominate the scene.

The role of the bureaucracy, in bringing about this situation, was very significant and must be mentioned. As the political sun of the Awami League rose ever higher on the horizon of East Pakistan, the bureaucrats were quick to link their fortunes with those of Sheikh Mujib and his henchmen. They surreptitiously helped the interests of the Awami League, and looked to Sheikh Mujib for guidance. They envisaged promotions and higher appointments in an independent Bangladesh. Even military officers forgot their oath of loyalty to defend Pakistan, envisaging quick promotions and a glittering future in the armed forces of an independent Bangladesh. The gains made by the bureaucracy and the armed forces, due to the emergence of Pakistan, were recent examples and still fresh in their minds.

The elections were preceded by the disastrous cyclone of November 1970, which will be dealt with later. Some fifteen constituencies were affected by the cyclone, and elections were postponed in those areas. However, the decision was taken to hold the elections on schedule in the rest of the province. As ordered, the armed forces stayed away from all the polling stations, and only the personnel of the Election Commission and the police were present there; the polling was generally peaceful. The opposition parties lay low while the Awami League, encouraged by the government agencies, held complete sway. The results were a foregone conclusion. Except for two seats, all the others were captured by the Awami League. The two exceptions were Nurul Amin, who was victorious from Mymensingh, and Raja Tridiv Roy, the Chakma Chief, who won his contest from the Chittagong Hill Tracts.

Elections in the cyclone-affected areas were held a few weeks later; all the Awami League candidates from those areas were elected. The Awami League leader and his party now showed their true colours. Sheikh Mujib was totally insufferable. During one of his visits to East Pakistan after the elections, President Yahya Khan, while talking to the press, referred to Sheikh Mujib as the future Prime Minister of Pakistan. This reference boosted Sheikh Mujib's ego no end. It was announced that the newly-elected National Assembly would meet in Dhaka on 3 March 1971, to elect the leader of the house and go through the various constitutional steps for the formation of a civilian government. However, before we proceed with these events, let us talk at some length about the cyclone of 1970.

Notes

1. 'My aim is to establish Bangladesh; I will tear the LFO [Legal Framework Order] into pieces as soon as the elections are over. Who could challenge me once the elections are over?' (Stanley Wolpert, *Zulfi Bhutto of Pakistan: His Life and Times*, Karachi: Oxford University Press, 2007, p. 141).
2. 28 March 1970: The Legal Framework Order was issued, outlining election procedures as well as considerations for the future government and the constitution. The country's original name, Islamic Republic of Pakistan, was restored while the One Unit was dissolved.

4

The Devastating Cyclone of November 1970

On the night between 12 and 13 November 1970, East Pakistan's coastline was struck by a major tragedy in the shape of a cyclone accompanied by tidal waves. It hit the territory in the Khulna area and swept the coastal areas all the way to Chittagong and beyond. Even in Dhaka, we experienced gale winds but no significant damage was done to property other than the uprooting of some trees. The communications in the affected areas were completely disrupted. Hence, there was a lack of reporting in the immediate aftermath. It was only two or three days later that news of the tragedy started trickling in. Initially, the civil administration committed an error of judgement and ignored the news. The Governor had convened a conference of deputy commissioners and superintendents of police and went ahead with it as if nothing had happened.

Perturbed by the indifference of the administration, I collected two of my brigade commanders and some of my staff officers, and took off in an MI8 helicopter. We flew over the affected area extensively, and touched down in several places to get first-hand accounts from the survivors. There were tales of woe and horror. Food stocks had been washed away and, everywhere, we were besieged by hungry people, in need of food and clothes. Hut dwellings, which constituted 99 per cent of the structures, had been completely wiped out. From the air, we spotted a very large number of human and animal corpses floating in the water. It was not possible to take a tally because the casualties were in the thousands. We concluded that immediate government intervention was required. On our return, I had a meeting with the Governor and advised him that the government should commence relief work immediately, calling the army in to assist. I said that my officers and men would be glad to participate in alleviating this national tragedy.

After consulting his staff, the Governor decided not to involve the army. He appointed Mr Anis-uz-Zaman as the Relief Commissioner, with the task of administrating relief in all the affected areas. The Bengali bureaucrats had decided to demonstrate that they were capable of looking after themselves, rather than turning to the much-hated Punjabi army for help. They forgot that half my men were Bengalis.

After my offer of help was ignored, I felt somewhat disgusted and left for a tour of the Sylhet area. I had been there for only a day when a special aircraft was sent to fetch me back to Dhaka. As soon as I landed at Dhaka I was besieged by the international press, who had converged on Dhaka and were looking for stories. I parried their questions and got down to organizational work. The area was divided into various convenient sectors, officers-in-charge were appointed, and the deployment of troops started immediately. The press had created such a degree of awareness about the situation that international aid started pouring in immediately. The most welcome were the detachments of helicopters from USA,

France, and Germany which were assigned to the different areas, particularly the offshore islands and those areas where communications had been disrupted by the tidal waves. A British naval task force from Singapore anchored off the coast of Patuakhali, south of Barisal, provided helicopters and assault boats. We gladly accepted reinforcement of a further detachment of helicopters as well. This combination worked well, and Lieutenant Colonel Babar took everybody under his wing and put together an efficient and effective team. Our own General Headquarters was put to shame by the rush of international aid.

Incidentally, President Yahya Khan was paying a visit to Nepal when East Pakistan was struck by the cyclone. He curtailed his visit and returned to Dhaka. He was visibly upset by the tragedy and decided to survey the affected areas aerially. Unfortunately, he was flown in a Fokker Friendship aircraft which flew at a safe height of over ten thousand feet. From this height, he could see few details and, therefore, swallowed the civil government's official version that not much damage had been done. When he reached Rawalpindi, he was embarrassed by the news carried by the international press. He flew back to Dhaka post-haste, but by then the Bengali press had spread enough poison: they had carried vastly exaggerated stories of the casualties and economic damage, and decried the relief efforts of the Central Government. Not one word of praise, for the efforts of the army, was published. It was a shameful and deliberate parochialism on the part of the East Pakistani press. I also remember that the people of Punjab, particularly from Lahore, donated generously to the victims of the cyclone. Not a word of gratitude was written, for these gestures, in the mainstream East Pakistani press.

Sheikh Mujib, and the rest of the Awami League leadership, had created such a deep chasm between the two wings of the country that any chance of bridging it seemed remote. It was no wonder that the Awami League won all the remaining seats. After this, Mujib became even more insufferable. He began to show his fangs openly to the President, and adopted an increasingly inflexible attitude when negotiating with Zulfikar Ali Bhutto and the Martial Law government. Instead of helping to bridge the gap, it helped increase the polarization.

5

A No-Win Situation

Even before the elections had taken place, the intellectuals of the Awami League had got down to work and prepared a new constitution for a united Pakistan, based on the Awami League's Six Points. Their leadership adopted this as the basis for future negotiations with the Martial Law government and the other political parties, particularly Zulfikar Ali Bhutto's Pakistan People's Party. Bhutto had won a decisive majority in West Pakistan, but not a single seat in East Pakistan. His party had not done its homework on framing a constitution. They just cashed in on their slogan of '*roti, kapra, aur makaan*'. The Awami League also had the support of some minor political parties of West Pakistan, although none of their candidates had been elected to the National Assembly from that province. However, even without them, the Awami League had an overall decisive majority in the National Assembly. Here was a situation of complete polarization between the two wings of Pakistan, unless the two major political parties reached an understanding and formed a national government. Bhutto was not prepared to sit on the Opposition benches and give Sheikh Mujib a chance to run the government alone which, in fact, was his due. Both parties adopted an inflexible attitude during their negotiations and the likelihood of collaboration receded. In the meantime, Sheikh Mujib held a rally at the Ramna Race Course on 3 January 1971. At the massive gathering, he got all the 417 newly-elected Awami League members of the National and Provincial assemblies to take an oath of loyalty to the Six and Eleven-Point programmes,[1] which were the basis of the party manifesto. This clearly indicated a victory of the hardliners and students who were well-known for their extremism.

On 12 January 1971, General Yahya Khan held a decisive meeting with Sheikh Mujib. Sheikh Mujib was not prepared to concede any ground and the President closed the meeting in disgust. He left Dhaka in some anger and went straight to Larkana where he was Bhutto's guest. There they were joined by General Abdul Hamid Khan. During the next two days, momentous decisions were taken about the fate of the country. A lot has been written about this meeting but it is all guesswork. The three participants are dead, and none of them went on record about this particular event; there is no official version either. However, one thing appears to be reasonably certain: the trio appeared to have reached an understanding about various issues. Certain events and attitudes provide sufficiently credible clues for that.

In order to pressurize both the parties, and to meet the constitutional deadline of 14 February, General Yahya Khan convened the National Assembly at Dhaka on 3 March 1971. As the deadline approached, neither one of the two main political parties showed any flexibility.

At this stage, it is pertinent to mention that during January and early February 1971, General Yahya had visualized the possibility of a military crackdown accompanied by the suspension of all political activity. He, therefore, prepared a plan called Operation Blitz, which was cleared with the headquarters of the Chief Martial Law Administrator and a copy provided to General Headquarters. I had shown this operation instruction to my brigade commanders and directed them to have detailed plans ready for their respective areas of responsibility. In their turn, they prepared their plans. In essence, Operation Blitz meant the suspension of all political activity in the country and a reversion to Martial Law rule. This meant that the armed forces of the country would be permitted to move against defiant political leaders and to take them into protective custody.

General Yaqub and the Governor had gone to attend a conference convened by the President. They returned on 25 February 1971. On 26 February, General Yaqub convened a Martial Law conference. As usual, it was attended by the sub-administrators and those of us in Dhaka. He informed us that the President was going to announce the *sine die** postponement of the National Assembly at midday on 1 March 1971. General Yaqub directed that we be ready to put Operation Blitz into action at short notice. I was also informed that 57 Brigade, ex 16 Division at Quetta, was already on the move to Karachi from where it would be ready to fly into Dhaka at a given codeword. I submitted that the concerned brigade's fly-in should be carried out immediately after arrival at Karachi. This would add to our deterrence value against the mischief mongers. This was readily agreed to, and the request granted by General Headquarters. The reader must remember that these reinforcements could not

---
* Indefinite.

carry their heavy weapons with them. Their usefulness against organized resistance was, therefore, very limited.

On 27 February 1971, I gave formal orders to my brigade commanders to be prepared to put Operation Blitz into action, at short notice, on a given codeword. This could be expected any time after midday on 1 March. As a result, troops moved out on 27 February to Khulna, Faridpur, Barisal, Bogra, Pabna, Mymensingh, and Tangail. Some troops were already located in Darsana, Benapole, Ghoraghat, and Brahmanbaria.

I was not part of the scenario, but I believe that Admiral Ahsan made some last-ditch attempts to save the situation and persuade the President not to postpone the meeting of the National Assembly scheduled for 1 March. The President did not agree and, instead, relieved Admiral Ahsan of his job. The President also appointed General Yaqub as the Governor of East Pakistan. He was already the Martial Law Administrator Zone 'B' and Commander Eastern Command. General Yaqub was thus elevated, but not for long as the march of events overtook everybody.

Since 1971, I have done some reading on the events of that period. Finally, I chose an article by Professor Rehman Sobhan, who is an eminent economist and was a close confidant of Sheikh Mujib, particularly on economic matters. His article provides an authentic version of the Bengali viewpoint, and how they saw the development of the situation up to the military action on 25 March 1971. Obviously, all of it is NOT true and authentic, but I feel it is a useful document and deserves inclusion in this book (Annexure A).

It is meant to give the reader a glimpse of the events from the other side. Professor Sobhan admits that some of the statements made by him are based on conjecture and may not necessarily be true. In the next chapter, I shall narrate events as I knew them. Therefore, the reader can draw his own conclusions.

Note

1. On 4 January 1969, leaders of the East Pakistan Students' Union (Menon Group), East Pakistan Students' League, East Pakistan Students' Union and a section of National Students' Federation (all part of the then Students' Action Committee) declared their Eleven-Point programme. The Eleven Points included the Six Points of Awami League as declared by Sheikh Mujibur Rahman, including provincial autonomy, the demands centring round students' own demands as well as the demands relating to the problems of the workers.
The Eleven Points were as follows:

    1. The state of the entire educational system. The demands of the students were also included in this first point. In fact seventeen items were presented in the form of demands in the first point, including the expansion of school and college education by increasing the number of schools and colleges and technical institutions, the reduction of school and college fees by 50 per cent, a food subsidy for the dining halls and canteen expenses, the introduction of education in the mother tongue at all stages, free and compulsory education up to class eight, the expansion of female education, an increase in the number of medical, agricultural, and technical colleges, universities, and institutions, travel subsidies to student in all forms of transport as was being extended to students in West Pakistan, guarantee of jobs, the cancellation of the black university ordinance and a guarantee of the autonomy of the universities and other educational institutions and the scrapping of the National Education Commission Report and the Report of the Hamoodur Rahman Commission.
    2. Direct election on the basis of adult franchise for establishing parliamentary democracy and ensuring the freedom of speech and of the newspapers.
    3. Full autonomy for East Pakistan within the framework of a Federal Constitution.
    4. Sub-federation in West Pakistan with regional autonomy for all provinces including Balochistan, North-West Frontier Province and Sindh.

5. Nationalization of banks and insurance companies, the jute trade and big industries.
6. Reduction of rents and taxes on peasants, remission of all area rents and loans, abolition of the certification system, etc.
7. Guarantee of fair wages and bonus for workers and provision for their education, housing, medical facilities; withdrawal of all anti-worker black laws and the granting of the right to strike and form trade unions.
8. Flood control and provision for proper use of water resources in East Pakistan.
9. Withdrawal of the Emergency Ordinance, Security Act and all Preventive Detention Acts.
10. Abrogation of SEATO, CENTO and Pak-American military pacts and formulation of a non-aligned and independent foreign policy.
11. Release of all students, workers, peasants and political leaders and activists from various jails of the country, and withdrawal of all warrants of arrest and cases, including the Agartala Conspiracy Case.

Source: Badruddin Umar, *The Emergence of Bangladesh, Vol. 2: Rise of Bengali Nationalism (1958–1971)*, Karachi: Oxford University Press, 2006, pp. 148–149.

6

The Crisis Deepens

It is important to dilate on certain matters and events prior to 1 March 1971 that had either a direct or an indirect bearing on events during the month of March 1971. At best, Martial Law rule in East Pakistan during 1969–71 was a very tame and diluted affair. All politicians of any consequence were undeclared 'holy cows'. They were not to be touched, according to verbal instructions from the Centre. We had certain knowledge that the assassins of my two non-commissioned officers were living with impunity in Jagan Nath Hall of Dhaka University. Many other wanted criminals were also hiding in the student hostels of the university. It was proposed, to the Chief Martial Law Administrator, that a surprise raid on these hostels would produce a good haul of criminals and individuals wanted by the law-enforcing agencies. The possibility of such a raid was rejected outright by the Chief Martial Law Administrator. In another incident, two rich Hindus were arrested. They owned tea estates and vast amounts of property yielding an income of millions of rupees. However, their bank accounts in East Pakistan showed only a few thousand rupees in them. The rest of their cash was lying safely in the banks in Calcutta. A summary military court sentenced them to six months' imprisonment along with the confiscation of their property. However, when the sentence was solemnly announced, they chided the court and declared that, in spite of the sentence of imprisonment, they would be spending the night in the comfort of their homes and not in jail. And how right they were, for orders came from the Chief Martial Law Administrator to release them forthwith! I have narrated these incidents to illustrate the serious erosion of Martial Law authority. It had turned into a toothless tiger. What made the situation even worse was that everybody concerned knew this.

We used to hold regular monthly meetings of the Intelligence Coordination Committee, presided over by the Governor. The Commander, Eastern Command, and I were members of this committee. The chiefs of the provincial intelligence reported to the committee as well. The emphasis was invariably on the past activities of the underground Communist and terrorist organizations which remained elusive. The government was always one step behind and never caught up with them.

During the pre-election year, the bureaucracy in East Pakistan had lined up with the Awami League and cast their lot with it. There was also a strong, public tidal wave in favour of the Awami League. It was not difficult to predict that the Awami League would sweep the board. However, the Chief Martial Law Administrator remained blind to the situation. His advisers and their reporting agencies kept him ignorant of the reality. He never consulted me, and my written word to General Headquarters and the headquarters of the Chief Martial Law Administrator was apparently never brought to his notice or, if he ever read it, he did not believe it. It is also possible that after having made the initial mistake, General Yahya Khan discovered that he could not solve the crisis.

In the western wing, Bhutto had won a strong majority and was threatening the President's base. Even the rank and file of the army came from a class which had lent strong support to Bhutto. It appears that General Yahya Khan was keen to strike a compromise with Bhutto, even if it was at the cost of Sheikh Mujib. It was too risky for the President to jeopardize the security of his own base and to cast his lot with Mujib instead. As he saw it, Mujib had already proved unreliable. Prior to the elections, Mujib had taken extraordinary care to appear meek and servile to General Yahya Khan. After the elections, Mujib's position was unassailable and he was very conscious of his new-found strength. The administration in East Pakistan was already looking to him for guidance and expected to receive instructions on all important matters of State from him. No one declared this openly, but nobody made a secret of it either. The Awami League had started flexing its muscles and began to prepare for a showdown with the Martial Law authority. Countless reports of military preparations had started to come in. Reports of Indian subversion and infiltration were equally numerous. Smuggling of arms from across the Indian border had become commonplace. Looting of arms' shops, even in the large cities, was on the increase. It was obvious that the Awami League, enjoying wide support, was getting ready for a face-to-face confrontation in the near future.

It will be recalled that despite the pleading of both Mujib and Governor Ahsan, the President had decided to postpone the National Assembly meeting which had previously been convened to meet in Dhaka on 3 March 1971. In a last-ditch attempt, it was proposed to the President that, when announcing the postponement, he should announce a new date not too far away. He, however, decided to make the postponement *sine die* as he felt that a new date in March 1971 was unlikely to allow him to be much nearer a solution between the two warring political parties. Therefore, he went ahead with his planned announcement on the morning of 1 March 1971. The news was electrifying to the common man in East Pakistan, and particularly so in Dhaka. In no time at all, there were crowds on the streets of Dhaka. Sheikh Mujib called a hurried press conference at the Hotel Purbani, and announced a province-wide strike. He announced that, on 4 March, he would lead a procession to Paltan Maidan where he would address a meeting. Having said this, he went into a session with the Awami League Working Committee at the hotel.

In response to Mujib's call for a general strike, something unprecedented happened. The entire province came to a grinding halt. The provincial civil administration, including the police, struck off work in obedience to Mujib's call. Awami League workers took to violence and made sure that the strike was a total success in all walks of life. Incidents of burning of the national flag and trampling on the Quaid-i-Azam's portraits were reported from various places. I do not know of another parallel example of such complete paralysis of civic life and administration in East Pakistan at that time. To illustrate this, I will narrate one small incident.

As a sequel to the November 1970 cyclone, the Central Government convened a committee to examine the system of weather-reporting, including the warning system for cyclones/storms. The committee had several members; I was appointed its Chairman. From the armed services, the committee included Air Vice Marshal Qadir, while Brigadier (later Major General) Mian Abdul Qayyum was appointed its Secretary with the task of compiling the report. He was provided with an office, and the necessary staff and equipment, in the premises of the Provincial Civil Secretariat. After his inclusion in the committee, he carried on with his normal duties. On 1 March 1971, he went to his office. Sometime before midday, I received a telephone call from a very agitated Brigadier Qayyum who described the situation saying that a large and unruly crowd had assembled in the secretariat premises shouting '*Joy Bangla*!'.* The officials and staff of the secretariat had closed shop and either joined the crowd or escaped home. The crowd had pulled down the Pakistan flag and set it on fire. Brigadier Qayyum's own staff had quietly disappeared, leaving him alone in this perilous situation. He naturally requested help in being evacuated from his unenviable predicament. I advised him to lock himself in and lie low till a rescue was organized. He kept calm and waited patiently for deliverance. Luckily, soon after that, the crowd thinned out and dispersed. Thus, Brigadier Qayyum was rescued without any bodily harm or application of force.

Going back a little bit, as the crisis began to deepen towards the end of February, Sheikh Mujib had been kept well informed about the goings on within the government. In fact, on the night between 28 February and 1 March, he already knew that President Yahya Khan would adjourn the proposed National Assembly meeting *sine die* in a few hours. Therefore, he and his party had plenty of time to plan their future course of action, and were ready and quick to exploit their initial success of 1 March.

---

* Victory to Bengal.

Mujib's house in the Dhanmandi area of Dhaka became the focal point of all political activity, and the Awami League high command went into continuous session there. Responsibilities were delegated for all functions of the government including the public utility services, banks, transportation, and the information media. The Martial Law Administrator, at this stage, was left with no one to answer his commands, except his troops. Even in the matter of troops, it became clear to us at this stage that the Bengali troops would not shoot at the Bengali crowds. In fact, it seemed obvious that on a clarion call from Sheikh Mujib, they would even take up arms in his support.

The unity of action and purpose demonstrated by the entire province was so complete that it could not possibly be felt and appreciated anywhere outside the province, especially in West Pakistan. One had to be there, on the spot, to see how effective it was. Even the buses and railway trains were left at wayside stations where they were deserted by their staff. The Dhaka airport staff also went on strike and disappeared. Late in the evening, I was informed that a PIA Boeing from the Western wing was half an hour away from Dhaka, while the airport had been plunged into total darkness. The plane had insufficient fuel to continue its journey to Rangoon. Therefore, in the absence of any landing facilities, it would have to land in Calcutta. I alerted Air Commodore Masood, who was Commander of the Pakistan Air Force Base. He acted with great alacrity and activated the airfield in time to receive the Boeing safely.

In view of the situation that had developed province-wide, on 1 March 1971, I had quick consultations with my senior staff and some commanders available in Dhaka regarding the feasibility of conducting Operation Blitz in the prevailing circumstances. Each one of them was of the opinion that it would be sheer 'lunacy' to attempt the operation at that time as the whole basis, and all the prerequisites, for attempting it successfully had been knocked out with one blow. The problem could only be solved politically now; any attempt at the use of force would divide both the wings forever, causing untold misery and bloodshed among the people.

Lieutenant General Yaqub Khan called me to his Martial Law headquarters in the new capital area. As far as I remember, the others present were Major General Rao Farman Ali Khan, Brigadier (later Lieutenant General) Ghulam Jilani Khan (Brigadier, Martial Law), Brigadier Ali El-Edroos (Chief of Staff at Command Headquarters), and Air Commodore Masood (Commander PAF, East Pakistan). All those present, including Yaqub Khan, were in unanimous agreement with the views expressed by my senior staff and commanders, as mentioned above. Yaqub felt that the President should visit Dhaka in person at the earliest, and take decisions that only he could take. New developments were taking place and changing so rapidly that the situation could no longer be handled by remote control from Rawalpindi. No other alternatives were proposed. Consequently, Yaqub started working towards this end and several messages, via telephone and in writing, were exchanged between him and headquarters of the Chief Martial Law Administrator at Rawalpindi. Apparently, the President was not convinced that his presence would help. He wanted Yaqub and his Eastern Command to fend for themselves and do their best. During the ensuing few days, this tug-of-war went on between the Commander Eastern

Command and the President through Lieutenant General S.G.M.M. Peerzada, the latter's Principal Staff Officer.

From 1 March onwards, the situation in East Pakistan became very fluid. Significant events were taking place by the hour and it was not easy to remain up to date. Instead of standing by in Karachi, the fly-in of troops had begun with effect from the night between 1 and 2 March. However, express orders were issued by Headquarters Eastern Command that no troops were to be sent to Dhaka city. Large crowds were moving about the city, singing nationalist songs and carrying Bangladesh flags. We wanted to avoid confrontation at all costs. However, late in the afternoon, the crowds went berserk and there were cases of looting and arson. Casualties were inflicted on the Biharis and West Pakistanis. By the evening, the situation had got completely out of hand. The Chief Secretary to the Governor, Mr Shafi-ul-Azam, and the Inspector General of Police, personally requested the deployment of troops in the city to put a stop to the looting and carnage. The troops were already standing by, ready for such a call, and they moved out quickly at 8:30 p.m. Although their progress was impeded by numerous road blocks, they had reached the affected area around Paltan Maidan by 9:30 p.m. Within two hours, an effective curfew had been imposed throughout the city. The troops stayed out in the city during the next few days. After law and order was fully restored, they were gradually withdrawn to the cantonment. A few light detachments were, however, left to guard vulnerable points like the State Bank, the Broadcasting House, and the television station.

Various segments of East Pakistanis, especially the Bengalis, acted with total unity on Sheikh Mujib's instructions. Many did so because they were afraid of reprisals and not because they were members of the Awami League itself. However, everybody was in line and complied as one man. The army supply contractors stopped supplying fresh rations to the troops. The troops had to do without this luxury, though they had the power to procure it for themselves. Restraining them on such an issue was not helping to foster their morale. I think that, at this time, resentment against the Bengali community had started to build up. This came to the fore when military action was eventually ordered on 25 March. On 26 March, I remember hearing slogans like 'General Raja *zindabad*!'* from troops returning to the cantonment from the city.

Problems of personnel administration were also seriously compounded for all of us. The local domestic staff at the Command House and the GOC's House evaporated all at once. The Governor's House was no exception. Admiral Ahsan was still there, trying to wind up. Suddenly, our supply of fresh rations dried up too. A sympathetic friend from West Pakistan flew in a basket of fresh fruits and vegetables, which was gratefully received and eagerly shared. A Punjabi friend, who could pass off for a Bengali, risked his life but managed to purchase some fresh vegetables in a civilian car. It was considered quite a coup.

The latest outbreak of violence in the city unnerved the civilian non-Bengalis, including a large number of students from West Pakistan studying at Dhaka University. There was

---
* Long live.

such a rush for buying air passages to West Pakistan that long queues began forming at the airport. Some Pathans were quick to cash in on this situation. They would stand in the queue and keep an individual's place for a sum of money while the individual went to attend a call of nature or buy himself some food. I directed my staff to make sense of the chaos at the airport and prevent black-marketing of air tickets. The army also organized what one might call a 'refugee camp' in the Adamjee College, in the cantonment. The cantonment, at the time, had become a place of refuge for many West Pakistani civilians waiting for an airlift including the families of industrialists like the Adamjees and Bawanys, as well as the students. My wife, Rafia, played a large part in housing the refugees and in arranging the return of many military families, along with some civilians, to West Pakistan in the troop-carrying aircraft. She even temporarily housed some thirty young students in the GOC's House. Many well-to-do people simply parked their expensive cars in the cantonment, and in some cases dumped the car keys with my guard at the residence. The situation caused a great deal of hardship to these civilians but there was no panic; it always remained organized and under control.

In the meantime, Lieutenant General Yaqub Khan continued to work for an early visit to Dhaka by the President. On the morning of 4 March 1971, when he appeared to be unsuccessful, Yaqub indicated to Lieutenant General Peerzada that in case the President's visit did not materialize, he would be left with no choice but to resign. All this happened while I was present in his office. We were soon joined by Major General Rao Farman. We both asked Yaqub to convey our resignations also. He, however, advised that we should not resort to collective action. Being the Senior Commander, it was his prerogative to resign in protest. The telephones continued to ring during the rest of the morning and further efforts were made to persuade the President to pay a visit to Dhaka. A telephone conversation between President Yahya Khan and Sheikh Mujib was also arranged. Shortly before we dispersed for lunch, the President agreed to come to Dhaka around 15 March. He said that his visit was not to be divulged and that Sheikh Mujib would get much more than he had asked for or had even expected. On that happy note, we heaved a sigh of relief and dispersed for lunch. As Farman and I were about to depart, Yaqub Khan asked both of us to join him for dinner along with our wives. Admiral Ahsan was also expected to be there as he was leaving for Karachi later that evening.

As it happened, Admiral Ahsan missed the dinner as he had left for Karachi by an earlier flight. However, I went to the Command House with my wife for dinner. The Farmans were already there. We went through the dinner somewhat solemnly and returned to the drawing room where green tea was served. As we were sipping tea, the telephone rang. The domestic staff member beckoned Lieutenant General Yaqub Khan to attend. Apparently, it was President Yahya Khan himself at the other end. We could hear our end of the conversation. It appeared the President had once again changed his mind and rescinded his earlier decision to come to Dhaka around 15 March. Lieutenant General Yaqub Khan earnestly pleaded with him not to do so. After a brief conversation, the President rang off. Yaqub Khan walked back to the drawing room with a heavy step, looking despondent. Before he returned to us, he asked the operator to connect him with Lieutenant General Peerzada at Rawalpindi. This was done in a short while. He informed Peerzada about his conversation with the President, told him that he was resigning from his post, and that the written resignation would be communicated on the morning of 5 March.[1]

After Lieutenant General Yaqub Khan had finished with the telephone call, we reassembled in the drawing room and started discussing the situation and our future course of action. The President's blunt refusal was difficult to comprehend. We felt that no written word could fully convey the situation then existing in East Pakistan because it had to be seen to be believed. We, therefore, decided to send Rao Farman to Rawalpindi to convince the President about the importance of his presence in Dhaka at such a critical moment. In a totalitarian regime, only the person at the top can take momentous and important decisions that are called for. An aircraft was leaving for Karachi at midnight, and Farman took that flight at very short notice. The rest of us, in Dhaka, were left waiting for the next move from Rawalpindi.

As promised, Sheikh Mujib did address a rally on 3 March. His tone was not acrimonious. In fact, it could be said that it was rather conciliatory. However, with every passing day, the Awami League tightened its grip on the administration in East Pakistan. The *de facto** position was that all organs of the East Pakistan government reported to Sheikh Mujib's headquarters for instructions. Even the Inspector General of Police had stopped coming to Martial Law headquarters, but had started reporting to Sheikh Mujib's residence and received

---

* Actual.

instructions from there. Shafi-ul-Azam, the Chief Secretary to the Governor, continued to pay his daily calls, but since he expressed his inability to carry out any instructions, these were merely a formality.

On the morning of 5 March, I went to my headquarters and dealt with the urgent matters awaiting my attention. At about 10 a.m., I went to Lieutenant General Yaqub Khan to follow up on the events of the previous day. After the customary exchange of greetings, he offered me a seat opposite him across the table. As I sat down, he opened his briefcase, pulled out a file cover, and put it in front of me without uttering a word. Within the folder was a document consisting of two foolscap pages of an army message pad. It was addressed to the headquarters of the Chief Martial Law Administrator. It began by explaining the situation in East Pakistan, how the control of administration had passed on to Sheikh Mujib who was now the *de facto* head of government and controlled all public life. It then went on to explain why it was necessary for the Chief Martial Law Administrator to be personally present in East Pakistan at that time. In view of the President's point blank refusal for this course of action, he felt unable to carry on with his duties and, therefore, tendered his resignation. He ended the signal (telegram) by saying, 'General Khadim Raja is in the picture.' After reading the signal, when I raised my head, Lieutenant General Yaqub Khan explained that he could not wait for me to see it and had, therefore, sent it to Rawalpindi first thing that morning. He then asked me about the constitutional aspect of the situation resulting from his move. I told him that he had to continue with his job until his resignation was accepted. When that happened, he would be directed to hand over charge to a successor who would be named by the Chief Martial Law Administrator. He agreed with my interpretation and decided to carry on until officially relieved.

Sheikh Mujib had, in the meantime, announced that he would address a public rally at the Ramna Race Course on 7 March 1971 at 4 p.m. He had promised to chart out the future course of action at that rally. In a sense, the occasion could provide him with the ideal opportunity to take the plunge and declare East Pakistan's independence as an independent state. There was also a power vacuum in the Martial Law set up in East Pakistan. Although Yaqub Khan was technically in command, as a result of his differences with the President, he had already submitted his resignation and was waiting to be relieved. A lot of responsibility rested on my shoulders as the next-in-command and I was very conscious of it. I believe Sheikh Mujib was aware of it too—that a lot now depended on my reaction to future developments. I had no personal relationship with him as we had barely met, and never exchanged a word.

On the afternoon of 6 March 1971, the Awami League Working Committee was reported to be in session at Sheikh Mujib's residence, considering the text of his speech for 7 March. I don't know what transpired but there were many extremists in the Awami League. In fact, it had been reported to us that several die-hard Communists had smuggled themselves into the Awami League, without actually changing their creed or convictions. They planned to erode Mujib's party from within. Moreover, the student wing was, by nature, volatile and explosive; they, too, were a strong pressure group within the party.

Early in the evening of 6 March, one of my senior staff officers, accompanied by a Bengali gentleman, came to my residence and asked to see me. The Bengali gentleman was introduced to me but, unfortunately, I do not remember his name and I don't seem to have recorded it either. He said that he was a close confidant of Sheikh Mujib who had sent him to plead with me. Sheikh Mujib's message, briefly, was that he was under great pressure from the extremists and student leaders within the party to declare unilateral declaration of independence during his public address on the afternoon of 7 March. Sheikh Mujib claimed that he was a patriot and did not want any responsibility for the break-up of Pakistan. He, therefore, wanted me to take him into protective custody and confine him to the cantonment. For this, he wanted me to send a military escort to fetch him from his Dhanmandi residence.

For the information of the reader, Sheikh Mujib's residence was very heavily guarded by armed Awami League volunteers. In addition to the continued presence of the Working Committee, there were scores of expectant Awami League workers and members of the press in and around the area of the house. Only a lunatic would take Sheikh Mujib's proposal at face value and plunge into action when disastrous results were sure to follow. As I saw it, Sheikh Mujib was probing my reaction in case he declared the unilateral declaration of independence during his public rally on 7 March. My response would be very relevant and so it was important for him to get a prior inkling, if possible.

After hearing Sheikh Mujib's message, I decided to use the full weight of my position to prevent the catastrophe that could take place on 7 March. I told the confidant that I was fully convinced that Mujib was a patriot, and that his role as a student leader in Calcutta during the movement and agitation for Pakistan was well known to me. Therefore, in my opinion, how could he demolish what he had helped to create? In a light-hearted vein, I added that Sheikh Mujib was welcome to be my honoured guest if he felt threatened; for that, since he knew the cantonment area well, all he had to do was drive straight to my residence—in which case he would not need an escort as he would be coming of his own free will.

Sheikh Mujib did not give up. He decided to try one more time. At 2 a.m. on the night between 6 and 7 March, I was woken up and informed that two guests, accompanied by some of my staff officers, were waiting in the drawing room to see me on an urgent matter. This time, there were two different East Pakistani gentlemen. Besides them, my senior staff officers, Colonel (later Brigadier) Saadullah Khan, Lieutenant Colonel (later Brigadier) Mohammad Taj, and Major Munawwar Khan of the Divisional Intelligence were also present. The two visitors were formally introduced as emissaries from Sheikh Mujibur Rahman. I am afraid I do not recall the names of either of the two, but I do recollect that I had previously heard of one of them as a public figure. One of them did all the talking, and was apparently the spokesman. He repeated the earlier story, but with greater emphasis this time, once again stressing the threat to Sheikh Mujib's person and the need to take him into protective custody. As before, I did not buy the story. However, I added a strong warning this time. I told the emissaries to inform Sheikh Mujib that, during his speech, I would have the army—armed with guns and tanks—standing by in the cantonment, ready to move immediately. I would also have arrangements in place to listen to Sheikh Mujib's speech directly from the Race Course. In case Sheikh Mujib attacked the integrity of the country and proclaimed the Universal Declaration of Independence, I would discharge my duty without hesitation and with all the power at my command. I would have the army march in immediately with orders to wreck the meeting and, if necessary, raze Dhaka to the ground. I impressed upon the emissaries that they should inform Sheikh Mujib that the consequences of indiscretion would be disastrous and the onus would be entirely on him. I advised Sheikh Mujib to keep the door open for further negotiations and avoid unnecessary bloodshed.

According to Professor Rehman Sobhan, saner elements carried the day and it was decided not to take the extreme step but to leave the door open for further negotiation. While the army was standing by in the cantonment, I listened directly to Sheikh Mujib's speech. His tone was conciliatory and he merely repeated the four earlier demands of his 4 March speech. Within a few minutes, the speech was over. Before the recalcitrant elements could raise a hue and cry, Sheikh Mujib had hurriedly left the stage. In fact, the whole event was a bit of an anti-climax, but I thanked Allah and heaved a sigh of relief.

I had recorded, briefly, the points made by Sheikh Mujib during his speech on 7 March. It will be useful to reproduce them for the reader:

(a) He called upon his followers not to do anything that may precipitate an already explosive situation.
(b) Together they should seek the cooperation of the army for the maintenance of law and order. However, if the

army shot innocent people in future, he would be the first to declare them an army of occupation.
(c) Pakistan must remain united and he was not seeking political separation.
(d) As elected leader of the majority, he expected the President to consult him in all major matters and decisions.
(e) They had to do all they could for the inter-wing hatred to die down.
(f) They must request West Pakistan not to treat them as a colony.
(g) They must bring to the notice of the world press the recent happenings in East Pakistan.

If we take into consideration President Yahya Khan's speech of the day before, i.e. 6 March, Sheikh Mujib's was remarkably conciliatory. President Yahya Khan had put all the blame for the crisis on Sheikh Mujib, and not even alluded to Bhutto. Hence, it was believed by most people that Sheikh Mujib would use the public meeting of 7 March to proclaim independence. The reasons have been mentioned, but credit goes to Sheikh Mujib for averting an immediate crisis and for preventing a lot of Bengali blood being spilt on the streets of Dhaka.

Note

1. 'I am convinced there is no military solution, which can make sense in the present situation. I am consequently unable to accept the responsibility for implementing a mission namely, military solution, that would mean civil war and large scale killings of unarmed civilians and would achieve no sane aim. It would have disastrous consequences.' (Anwar Dil, ed., *Strategy, Diplomacy, Humanity: Life and Work of Sahabzada Yaqub*, Intercultural Forum, Takshila Research University, 2005), pp. 280–284.

7

Lt. Gen. Tikka Khan in Action

President Yahya Khan had chosen Lieutenant General Tikka Khan, as the replacement for Lieutenant General Yaqub Khan, to head the Eastern Command. Tikka Khan had made a name for himself because of his numerous successes in the field. He had landed hard on the Baloch tribes who had raised their heads in revolt, causing them to lay down their arms or flee the country. Later, he punished the Indian troops who had intruded and occupied some of our territory in the Rann of Kutch, expeditiously evicting them with attendant loss of face. Later, during the 1965 War, he took command of the Sialkot Sector at a critical juncture. He stabilized the situation and then counter-attacked to retrieve some of the lost territory. With this military background, Tikka Khan was known to be a stern man of action and few words. His induction was not a very conciliatory gesture on the part of the President. It appeared that there was a change in the President's policy. He was replacing the 'doves' with the 'hawks' in East Pakistan.

Lieutenant General Tikka Khan arrived quietly at Dhaka airport on 7 March 1971 at 4 p.m., accompanied by Major General Rao Farman who had led the abortive mission to the President. Yaqub and I went to receive him at the airport. As we walked from the aircraft to the waiting cars, Tikka Khan remarked to me, 'Khadim, what the hell has your Division been doing all this time? There is such a bloody mess out here.' I felt angry at this rather ignorant and crude remark. I retorted, 'Now that you are here, you will soon find out for yourself.' This was not a happy beginning between my new boss and me. Just before we left the airport, it was decided that Lieutenant General Yaqub Khan would leave Dhaka on the evening of 8 March. I invited everybody present for a quiet farewell meal, at my residence, on the evening of his departure. Lieutenant General Tikka Khan cut me short and retorted that the farewell meal would be held at the Governor's House instead. I politely pointed out to him that it would not be possible for him to host the dinner at the Governor's House. But, as he insisted, I dropped the matter saying that he was welcome to go ahead with his proposal but *dal roti** would be ready at my residence, should he find it convenient.

Next day Tikka Khan found out that Chief Justice B.A. Siddiqui had bluntly declined to administer the Governor's oath of office to him. He pointed out that while we were birds of passage in that land, he and his family had to live there in the years to come. Tikka Khan also got to know that he had to stay in the Command House since the staff and servants at the Governor's House had all deserted. Needless to say, in the end, we all partook of *dal roti* as per my initial invitation.

Like most senior army officers, even at General Headquarters, Lieutenant General Tikka Khan was ill-informed about the

---
* Figurative term for a meal. Literally, lentil soup and unleavened flat whole wheat bread.

situation in East Pakistan. He had never served in East Pakistan. At best, his knowledge of the province was superficial and was based on the odd visit as the Quartermaster General while at General Headquarters. He obviously had a negative approach towards those of us who were at the helm of affairs or in senior positions in East Pakistan at the time. I do not think he realized that this time he had been given an impossible mission. He had no political mandate whereas the problem was inherently political and would not lend itself to a military solution. The Bengalis were, this time, determined to win their inalienable rights. And, if these were not granted, then they would not stop short of independence. Numerous opportunities presented themselves to the authorities but the bias remained in favour of applying force. This approach was doomed to failure in the long term.

Tikka Khan had two principal subordinates to deal with. I was in command of the troops while Farman dealt with civil affairs. Brigadier Mohammad Hussain Ansari, in command of the logistics, arranged logistic support for the fighting troops. All four of us belonged to the regiment of artillery and were, therefore, well known to each other. Our start was not as smooth as it should have been. However, events were moving so rapidly that there was no time to be lost. Within a week, all the rough edges had been smoothed out and we emerged as an effective and cooperative team. We had our honest differences now and again which were freely discussed during our frequent meetings and conferences. Invariably, the boss had the final say and the rest of us accepted it without rancour or malice even when convinced that it was not necessarily the best course of action. Our un-stinted cooperation led to quick military success but, I am sad to say, it was only temporary in nature and did not resolve the real issues which ultimately divided us as a nation.

In those early days of March 1971, the fly-in of troops into Dhaka from West Pakistan continued. PIA's fleet of Boeings flew the troops in. India had banned over-flights of Pakistani aircraft, an embargo I had anticipated and mentioned to General Abdul Hamid Khan months earlier. The 9 Division from Quetta, under Major General Nazar Hussain Shah, and 17 Division from Kharian, under Major General Shaukat Riza, were being flown in. The capability was limited—it being an eight-hour flight one-way—and, therefore, it took most of March and part of April 1971. Moreover, the troops arrived with personal or light weapons only. This seriously impaired their fighting capability with India, when the latter openly invaded East Pakistan in December 1971.

At the beginning of Tikka Khan's induction as head of the Eastern Command, the President's policy stipulated that the troops had to be confined to the cantonments and nothing was to be done to provoke an incident. Small detachments of troops were left to guard the State Bank of Pakistan, Radio Pakistan, and Dhaka Television Station; the rest of the troops in Dhaka had been withdrawn to their barracks. As mentioned earlier, the East Pakistanis had withdrawn all local administrative support to the army. Even the staff of the Military Engineering Service and the Cantonment Board had stopped working. The troops had to live on dry rations, which was very trying, and all kinds of rumours were afloat.

The most disturbing aspect of the overall situation was that the Bengali troops were seething with revolt, and widespread mutiny seemed to be in the offing. This would have provoked a civil war situation which we wanted to avoid at all cost. I, therefore, decided to quickly visit as many military stations as possible. The idea was to instil mutual confidence among the troops hailing from both wings of Pakistan. Therefore, I started my visit by meeting 2 East Bengal Regiment stationed at Joydebpur outside Dhaka. This unit was reported to be restive. My worst fears were confirmed because, as soon as my helicopter touched down, a large crowd of civilians from the bazaar collected. I was received by the Acting Commanding Officer and we collected in the officers' mess where I addressed the officers of the battalion. I explained the prevailing situation to them in order to counter any rumours and put their minds at rest. After this, I went round the troops who were busy in individual training on the open ground in front of the palace of the one-time Hindu raja. A large crowd had collected on the perimeters of the ground and kept booing as I went around with my entourage. I tried to be unmindful, as the circumstances warranted. The crowd remained outside the perimeter but the troops made no attempt to chase anybody away. After going through the inspection, I flew back to Dhaka. This visit further convinced me that the Bengali troops were on the verge of revolt and that we were sitting on a powder keg.

I decided to make a whirlwind tour of the rest of the military stations in the province. I managed trips to Jessore, Comilla, Chittagong, Sylhet, and Rangpur where I addressed gatherings of officers. I think, at least partly, I succeeded in clearing their misgivings and their anxieties. Resultantly, my command held together until we pressed the trigger first. There were no significant cases of insubordination or mutiny before

25 March. But, anxiety was written on most faces. There were numerous cases of desertion among Bengali troops, including one Subedar* and his batman of the Signal Battalion.

Tikka Khan had settled down for barely a week when the President arrived on 15 March. Besides the rest of his advisers and entourage, General Abdul Hamid Khan also accompanied him. The President called a conference the evening he arrived. I was present and explained the details of the prevailing situation. Not many people spoke although there were some comments and suggestions. Air Commodore Masood, Commander of the Air Force, then took the floor and spoke vehemently against military action as the solution. He pointed out that there were large numbers of Bihari settlers, and a significant number of West Pakistanis, whose lives and property would be jeopardized by such an action. The President had to take full responsibility for their honour, lives, and property. Air Commodore Masood spoke with a great deal of emphasis and emotion. There was pin-drop silence during his speech. The President finally intervened and stated that he was conscious of it all and hurriedly closed the meeting. In a few days, Air Commodore Masood was relieved by Air Commodore (later Air Marshal) Inam-ul-Haque. Air Commodore Masood was prematurely retired after a few weeks. This was a sad end to the career of a brilliant airman who had a reputation for skill and gallantry throughout the Pakistan Air Force, and among the rest of us who had known him.

---

* During Mughal times this term referred to a governor of a province. Later, it was used to refer to the chief native officer of a company of Indian soldiers in the British service. Before 1947, subedars were known as Viceroy's Commissioned Officers. After 1947, this term was used for Junior Commissioned Officers.

On 16 March, President Yahya Khan went into negotiations with Sheikh Mujib, who was assisted by his team of party advisers. The official statement in the press the next day was woolly, as is usual on such occasions. I happened to meet Lieutenant General Tikka Khan in the afternoon and asked him how the negotiations were going. In all simplicity, he replied that he knew only as much as I did from the daily newspapers. I was alarmed and requested him to visit the President's House and keep himself abreast of the happenings. I emphasized that there were no contingency plans to meet the present situation. In any case, I needed a lot of time to plan and give out orders so that action could be taken throughout the province in a coordinated manner. I also told him how General Yaqub Khan and Admiral Ahsan had separately told me that President Yahya Khan never confided in them but consulted his advisers instead. It was a strange phenomenon that the President should ignore his top men in East Pakistan and act on the advice of his inner coterie.

At about 10 p.m. on 17 March, I received a call from Lieutenant General Tikka Khan asking Major General Farman and me to go over to the Command House to see him. Some days earlier, Farman and his wife had left the Governor's House and were living with us in the cantonment. We both went and found that General Abdul Hamid Khan was also present. Tikka Khan informed us that the negotiations with Sheikh Mujib were not proceeding well and the President, therefore, wanted us to be ready for military action and to prepare a plan accordingly. No further verbal or written directions were issued. We were told to plan together and discuss the plan with the two dignitaries on the evening of 18 March.

On the morning of 18 March 1971, Farman and I assembled in my office to work on the plan. I had arranged that my wife would keep our Bengali ADC busy and away from my office. I did not want to arouse his suspicions about Farman working with me in my office the whole morning as it was a very unusual get-together in that environment. Short of time, we agreed on the broad details of the plan. Then we sat down to write our respective pieces. Farman was to supervise the operations of the Dhaka garrison while I was responsible for the rest of the province. He, therefore, wrote the preamble and how the operations were to be conducted in Dhaka. For the rest of the province, I detailed the troops to their respective tasks. As arranged, we met again at the Command House on the evening of 18 March. Finally, I presented the preamble and the plan. The plan was approved without any discussion. However, the 'deception' involving the President, visualized by us, was overruled because the President had his own plan—to flee from Dhaka prior to the military action.

On 21 March, Mr Bhutto arrived with his party advisers and lieutenants. We got news of his arrival just a day earlier. The Martial Law staff—Brigadier (later Lieutenant General) Ghulam Jilani Khan and others—looked into the security and accommodation for Bhutto and his entourage. They consulted Lieutenant General Peerzada, the President's Principal Staff Officer, who remarked that since Bhutto and his companions were politicians, they did not warrant official protocol, and should make their own arrangements upon their arrival in Dhaka. Leaving Bhutto and his party in the lurch like this, was fraught with danger. Bhutto could have been lynched in the prevalent mood—a move which would have set West Pakistan on fire. Consequently, we made arrangements to receive Bhutto, arranged for his lodging at the Inter-Continental Hotel, and providing security for him during his stay. Brigadier Jahanzeb Arbab, the Garrison Commander for Dhaka, was to make necessary arrangements along these lines and personally ensure Bhutto's safety. Brigadier Arbab was later rewarded by a grateful Bhutto with the rank of Lieutenant General and command of Bhutto's home province. As a matter of interest, Sheikh Mujib, acting as the *de facto* ruler, had offered to receive and host Bhutto. Protection was to be provided by volunteers of the Awami League. However, we felt that those arrangements were not foolproof and decided not to take a chance.

On their arrival, Bhutto and his party were driven to the hotel with a strong military escort. Troops were stationed at the hotel and at Farm Gate, *en route*, which was a notorious rendezvous for undesirable crowds and ruffians. Bhutto was thus able to join the negotiations, play his part, and return to West Pakistan safely.

The attention of the reader is drawn to the fact that the two top political leaders of the country, as well as the President and Chief of Army Staff, were locked in fruitless negotiations under the one roof. The two politicians had taken up extreme positions and there was little prospect of compromise between them. The President had apparently planned a role for himself in the future political set up as well. An observer on the sidelines could easily see that the negotiations were doomed to fail—a frustrating situation for those of us who were close to the events. In those tense circumstances, someone who trusted me completely approached me in confidence. This person, who I do not want to name, suggested that we should take the military and political leadership, assembled in Dhaka at that time, into custody and assume control of the country. The people and the country needed the honest and selfless leaders that we could provide them with. I took the suggestion as seriously as it was given, and promised to think it over. I pondered it overnight, without even confiding in my wife. Next morning, when I got ready to work, I had made up my mind. I had decided against the proposal and that I would continue with my work in the line of duty. Looking back, I feel happy that I retained my sense of balance and did not fall prey to temptation. It was not due to lack of courage; I must confess that my life has been governed by a degree of fatalism. I have never had a burning desire or ambition to strive for the pinnacle. My prayers have been confined to a happy family life, and an honest and decent living.

The new plan, prepared by Farman and myself, was named 'Searchlight'. There was no particular significance to its name. We were now ready with the plan and were waiting for orders to implement it. The problem we faced was how we were to convey it to the subordinate commanders without compromising security. There were various constraints. As there was not enough time and negotiations were barely dragging on, we had to get on with things quickly so that all the relevant elements were ready for action throughout the province. It was decided that I should proceed to Comilla and Chittagong to give orders to Brigadier Iqbal Shafi and Lieutenant Colonel Fatemi, respectively, commanding 20 Baluch. I was to give minimum details to Colonel Shigri, second-in-command of the East Bengal Regimental Centre, Chittagong, and to Lieutenant Colonel Janjua, commanding 8 East Bengal, also at Chittagong. To complicate matters,

Major General Eftikhar Khan Janjua, the Master General of Ordnance at General Headquarters, along with three staff officers, decided to take a lift with me. He was not aware of Operation Searchlight because the information was restricted on a 'need to know basis'. Brigadier Ansari, Commander of the Logistic Area, accompanied us. He was required to organize the unloading of MV 'Swat', by the troop labour, at Chittagong. MV 'Swat' was carrying seven thousand tons of ammunitions, which was the normal re-supply to maintain the reserves for three months in East Pakistan. In the charged atmosphere of suspicion, after the postponement of the National Assembly session, the Awami League appealed to the dock labour to boycott the offloading of the ship. The response was instantaneous and complete. The ship stood idle on the jetty for some weeks.

Before leaving for Chittagong, I discussed the situation regarding Brigadier M.R. Mozumdar, Commandant of the East Bengal Regimental Centre in Chittagong. Brigadier Mozumdar was the highest-ranking Bengali officer in East Pakistan. Bengali officers in the province, particularly unit commanders, looked to him for guidance. He had become the focal point of Bengali military activity and aspirations. Chittagong was our Achilles' heel. It was located on a major inlet from the sea, and had become all-important when India banned flights over its territory. Chittagong had a large military garrison, but the only West Pakistani troops stationed there belonged to the 20 Baluch Regiment who were on their way to West Pakistan. I believe 7 officers and 200 men had already departed, as the advance party, prior to the crisis. As this truncated battalion would, therefore, be wholly inadequate to hold Chittagong and keep the port open, we decided that I should play a little ruse and bring Brigadier Mozumdar back with me.

With this rather complicated and dicey mission, I set off for Comilla. I told Brigadier Ansari to take Major General Eftikhar Janjua and his party to see the ammunition dumps and other ordnance installations at the station. I sent for Lieutenant Colonel Mohammed Yaqub, commanding the 53 Field Regiment, to join Brigadier Iqbal Shafi for my briefing. I was able to brief them thoroughly. As per plan, Brigadier Shafi was to lead a strong column from his brigade and take control of Chittagong. Lieutenant Colonel Yaqub Malik, with his regiment and the remaining West Pakistani troops, was to control Comilla town and the surrounding areas.

I was reasonably satisfied with my briefing at Comilla. I then proceeded to Chittagong with my passengers. On arrival, I told Brigadier Mozumdar to accompany Brigadier Ansari and help him organize the offloading of MV 'Swat'. I also told him that 2 East Bengal Regiment at Joydebpur was a little restive in the absence of a proper commanding officer; in view of this, he should accompany me to Dhaka and talk to the officers and men in the capacity of 'Papa Tiger'. He felt elated and important and, from then onwards, there was no difficulty with him. At Dhaka, he was taken under protective custody and later moved to West Pakistan where he remained until repatriation.

The briefings at Chittagong were complicated. It was important to brief Lieutenant Colonel Fatemi of 20 Baluch fully because he had West Pakistani troops under his command who would be required to take action. Colonel

Shigri, of the East Bengal Regimental Centre, and Lieutenant Colonel Janjua were helpless in their command of Bengali troops. However, it was important that they knew enough to protect themselves, their West Pakistani colleagues, and their families. I drove over to Fatemi and gave him a thorough briefing. I could only steal a few moments with Colonel Shigri. Not being very sharp, he was somewhat baffled by my remarks; their significance dawned on him only some days later when Brigadier Iqbal Shafi arrived in Chittagong with his column and assumed control. Shigri was able to protect himself, but Janjua was not so fortunate. His second-in-command, Major (later General and President of Bangladesh) Zia-ur-Rahman, organized his killing along with that of two other West Pakistani officers of the battalion.

The passage of orders elsewhere was a simple affair. As I left for Comilla, Farman took off for Jessore and passed on the instructions to Brigadier Durrani, Commander of 107 Brigade. The next day, I was to proceed to Rangpur and Rajshahi whereas Farman was to proceed to Sylhet. However, Tikka Khan detained both of us in Dhaka, to deal with any possible emergency. Instead, we dispatched Colonel Saadullah Khan to Rangpur and Rajshahi. Saadullah Khan carried out his mission and dropped Lieutenant Colonel Shafqat Baluch, Commanding Officer of 27 Punjab, at Rajshahi. Brigadier Ali El-Edroos flew to Sylhet and briefed Lieutenant Colonel Sarfaraz Malik, who was commanding the 32 Punjab Regiment. No written orders for Operation Searchlight were issued. It was implemented on verbal orders. However, I have my personal copy which is attached as Annexure B for the benefit of the interested readers. The orders provided guidelines only; a lot was left to the individual commanders and their initiative. There were serious failures in Rajshahi and the Chuadanga area of Jessore Sector. Commanders in these areas failed to appreciate that they were dealing with a situation of insurgency. Apparently, their minds were fixed on 'aid to Civil Power', with which they were used to dealing during the past two or so years. Although this resulted in unnecessary casualties, the responsible officers got away with only premature retirement.

8

Operation Searchlight

The troops were stationed in eight permanent and temporary cantonments spread all over the province: Dhaka, Comilla, Chittagong, Sylhet, Jessore, Rajshahi, Saidpur, and Rangpur. In addition, 2 East Bengal Regiment was based in Joydebpur, a few miles outside Dhaka. As the crisis deepened in East Pakistan, I felt apprehensive about the East Bengal battalions which were part of each brigade. The 1 East Bengal Regiment was in Jessore, the 2 East Bengal outside Dhaka, the 3 East Bengal Regiment was in Saidpur near Rangpur, the 4 East Bengal Regiment in Comilla, the 8 East Bengal Regiment in Chittagong, and the 10 East Bengal Regiment was being raised in Dhaka, right next door to my headquarters. On one pretext or the other, I moved them out of their permanent locations and split them further into company groups, etc. Thus, they lost their ability for cohesive action until much later, when they broke out into open revolt and concentrated as battalions. This bought us some badly needed and invaluable time.

The critical elements of the plan were:

(a) Any act of insurgency was to be treated as open rebellion and dealt with accordingly with an iron fist.
(b) The element of surprise and deception was of paramount importance to ensure success. We even suggested that

the President be requested to help in the deception and be part of it.
(c) Bengali troops and police were to be disarmed as part of the plan. Of particular importance was the taking possession of the *kotes** of the East Pakistan Rifles in Peelkhana, the Reserve Police in Rajarbagh, and the armoury of some twenty thousand rifles in Chittagong before they could be distributed among the rebels.
(d) All external and internal communication was to be closed down at the beginning of the operation. These would be reopened, selectively, under our own control.
(e) The student halls of Dhaka University were to be surrounded and thoroughly searched for arms and wanted criminals.
(f) Sheikh Mujib was to be captured alive. Houses of some fifteen important Awami League and Communist Party leaders were to be searched, and these individuals taken into custody if found.

All hopes of a breakthrough in the negotiations had been abandoned. I was instructed to put Operation Searchlight into action on the night between 25 and 26 March 1971. The 'go ahead' signal was given soon after midday on 25 March. This was a momentous decision and I was very sad for the country. The supreme authority had decided to plunge the country into civil strife; the end result was a foregone conclusion. The Indian master strategist, Subramanyam, called it 'one chance in a millennium' to undo Pakistan. I was left amazed at the nonchalant way in which this decision was taken, almost light-heartedly. The President had apparently decided to dump East Pakistan and let it go its own way. He seemed to

---
* Unit armouries.

be concerned about his personal safety only. Therefore, he left Dhaka under some sort of a cover plan at about 7 p.m. on 25 March, which fooled nobody except, probably, himself. I tried to look as fresh and normal as possible.

At teatime, Major General Farman and I stepped out onto the lawn to join our wives who were waiting under the Bara Dari.* We were sipping tea when Kala Chand was announced. His arrival was sudden and without prior appointment. However, we let him join us. After some routine business conversation with the ladies, he turned to me and sought permission to make a submission. He said that, in the past, Dhaka had suffered its share of riots and lawlessness. In such situations, the previous GOCs had invariably provided him with guards and looked after his shop and family. I chided him for being unnecessarily panicky. He looked frightened and was almost trembling with fear. Seeing his miserable plight, I tried to calm him down and assure him about his safety. He soon left, but was still fearful.

I have narrated this episode to illustrate what an ill-guarded secret this portentous and explosive situation was. I think even the common man in the street was expecting the imminent 'crackdown'. Later that evening, Farman and I, accompanied by our wives, went to the Garrison Cinema and found that the hall was full of officers and their families. The attendance was normal. At the interval, when the lights were switched on, we were surprised to find that all the Bengalis had left the cinema's premises along with their families. The departure of the President, and its implication—that negotiations to solve the current crisis had failed—was, after all, not a well-kept secret.

---

* An elegant *nawabi*-style pavilion with twelve doors.

Soon after the President's departure, barricades and road-blocks started coming up on the streets of Dhaka. By now, the average resident was a professional at this game of blocking the roads. The troops, however, got into readiness in their barracks. Apart from the normal infantry, we had activated a troop of PT76 tanks. We also had some 106 mm recoilless rifles standing by for hard targets. The use of artillery was ruled out. Lieutenant Colonel Z.A. Khan of the 3 Commando Battalion, with some forty men, was standing by to accomplish his mission of taking Sheikh Mujib alive. For me, the wait was tortuous. In the interest of maintaining normalcy, I stayed at home till the action had begun. My headquarters had been fully activated and was functional. At about midnight, Brigadier Iqbal Shafi from Comilla called up. He informed me that his column was ready to take off for Chittagong. However, his Intelligence had reported that two wooden bridges near Feni, on the way to Chittagong, had been burnt down and a major obstacle created in his way. I told him to launch his column and make for Chittagong as soon as possible. It was vital that we take the town and keep the port open for resupply.

A little break from these depressing events: A few days earlier, Major General Farman and I had sent our children, and the West Pakistani domestic help, back to Lahore in one of the empty planes returning there after dropping the troops off. We had arranged a little codeword with my daughter, Rubina, who was an MA student at Dhaka University. Sheikh Mujib was to be referred to as '*mynah*'* whenever we talked with our children in Lahore on the telephone. We forgot that we actually had a pet *mynah* in the GOC's House, which a kind friend had sent us from Sylhet. On the night between 25 and

---

* A bird of the starling family (Sturnidae).

26 March, Lieutenant Colonel Z.A. Khan was successful in arresting Sheikh Mujib without many casualties. Sheikh Mujib was unhurt and safely lodged in a girls' school close to the GOC's House. To minimize the number of guards, I moved him to the guestroom of the Command House. Late at night, some heavy weapons were used against some hard targets. The *mynah* apparently had a weak heart, and unable to bear the boom of tank guns and recoilless rifles, succumbed to their noise. My wife rang Rubina up to give her a hint of the military action. Forgetting the secret meaning of the codeword, *mynah*, she told her that the poor *mynah*—referring to the bird—had expired. Despite it being late at night, news was flashed among the family in Lahore, that Sheikh Mujib had been killed. However, the official media the next morning came out with the correct news: Sheikh Mujib was safe and in the custody of the authorities.

Reports began coming in on the morning of 26 March. The operation had gone well in Dhaka. The East Pakistan Rifles in Peelkhana, and the Reserve Police in Rajarbagh, had been disarmed with less than ten casualties on both sides. However, there was a good bit of resistance from the University Halls, including the use of rifle and automatic fire. Consequently, to minimize casualties, the troops pressed the recoilless rifles and the troop of PT76 tanks into service. Thus, Dhaka was brought under control and calm prevailed in the city by early morning.

In Jessore, elements of the 1 East Bengal Regiment had apparently been forewarned and, after a brief fire-fight, left the cantonment with their heavy weapons. However, the company sent to Chuadanga by the Brigade Commander, on his own initiative, ran into serious trouble. They were taken by surprise and surrounded by the rebel Bengali troops. Ultimately, they were decimated and only a few succeeded in reaching the safety of Jessore town. The town of Jessore itself had also fallen into the hands of the rebels who, in addition, had the airport and runway under fire. Some Indian Border Security Forces had also crossed the border at Benapole and advanced some fifteen miles towards Jessore.

In Sylhet, 31 Punjab, under Lieutenant Colonel Sarfaraz Malik, had kept the airport secure by holding on to the surrounding hills. In Khulna, the Commanding Officer acted firmly and maintained good control over a difficult situation. In Rajshahi, the Commanding Officer, Lieutenant Colonel Shafqat Baluch, acted with a lack of judgement. He was not mindful of the 25 per cent Bengali inductees in his battalion. To make matters worse for himself, he sent half of his battalion to Pabna under a Bengali second-in-command. The net result was that the Bengali element of his unit deserted along with their arms. Ultimately, out of the 150 or so Punjabi soldiers at Pabna, all were killed except about 20 who managed to escape back to Rajshahi. The rebels surrounded the camp at Rajshahi; even the airship came under mortar and machine-gun fire. It became very difficult to reinforce the Rajshahi garrison, even by helicopter. Ultimately, I had to relieve Shafqat Baluch, who had won a *Sitara-e-Jurat*[*] at the Lahore front during the 1965 War; he was retired prematurely.

In Rangpur, Brigadier (later Major General) Abdullah Malik acted with wisdom and kept his cool. He started developing operations to capture Lal Monirhat airfield. He overcame the resistance there, which later helped us to reinforce North

---

[*] Star of courage. This is the third highest military award of Pakistan.

Bengal. The 29 Cavalry, equipped with PT76 tanks, was a composite unit with a 50 per cent Bengali component. We had weakened the remaining 50 per cent by activating a tank troop at Dhaka. It was the only major unit at Rangpur. Its Commanding Officer, Lieutenant Colonel (later Lieutenant General) Saghir Hussain Syed, acted with tact and managed to disarm the 50 per cent Bengali element of his unit without firing a shot. At Saidpur, two battalions were housed in a temporary encampment. The Frontier Force Battalion there was commanded by Lieutenant Colonel (later Major General) Hakim Arshad Qureshi, and the 3 East Bengal Regiment by Lieutenant Colonel (later Lieutenant General and President of Bangladesh) Hussain Mohammad Ershad. After a brief exchange of fire, the Bengali battalion moved out of the camp with their weapons, without putting up further resistance.

In Comilla, Lieutenant Colonel Yakub Malik acted with vigour and kept the situation well under control. The 4 East Bengal Regiment was located at Brahmanbaria in the north, on the road to Sylhet. The second-in-command, Major Khalid Musharraf, an East Pakistani, acted with decency. When the situation became well-known, he decided to assume command of the unit from his Commanding Officer, Lieutenant Colonel Malik who, along with the two other West Pakistani officers, was taken under protective custody. He finally handed them over to the Indian army at Agartala with the request that they should be treated properly as prisoners of war and returned safely to Pakistan at the end of hostilities. After the war, Lieutenant Colonel Malik was all praises for Major Khalid Musharraf.

The reports from Chittagong were discouraging. I have already referred to the place as our Achilles' heel. Chittagong was necessary for our survival—for us to keep the port open along with its communications to the hinterland. The 20 Baluch had moved according to plan and, after a fire-fight, managed to capture the armoury of the East Bengal Regimental Centre together with their ammunition dump. Then they started advancing towards the city but encountered heavy opposition when they approached the railway crossing. Major Zia-ur-Rahman had already disposed of his Commanding Officer together with two other West Pakistani colleagues. He took up a defensive position and isolated the town from the cantonment. The city was thus left, largely, in the hands of the rebels. Lieutenant Colonel Chaudhary, Chief Instructor of the East Bengal Regimental Centre, was known to be a staunch Awami League activist and proved himself so. He had organized two machine gun nests in his bungalow.

The navy was commanded by Commodore Mumtaz who faced acute problems. The naval base had at least 50 per cent Bengalis who, in many cases, held important positions. They were not yet disarmed and lived with the rest in a camp outside the town on the road to the airport. The Naval Communication Centre was located in the town, at Tiger Pass, not far from the Circuit House. It was a small detachment and very vulnerable in that location. Being static, it could not be moved.

We had lost contact with Brigadier Iqbal Shafi's column, whose location was not known. They were between Feni and Chittagong, where the demolished bridges and rebel troops had brought them to a halt.

On 26 March, after hearing all the reports, I decided to pay a visit to Chittagong to assess the situation personally and to take adequate steps. The trip to Chittagong was by a MI8 helicopter which was long overdue for overhaul. Although we were fired upon from the adjacent hills as we came down to land among the 20 Baluch lines, fortunately we were not hit. Lieutenant Colonel Fatemi briefed me as well as he could about the situation. Unfortunately, the airport had been captured and was controlled by rebel troops from the East Pakistan Rifles. The Naval Communication Centre in Tiger Pass was under fire from the adjoining hills. Being a small detachment, they were in serious difficulties. The men of 31 Punjab's company, who had helped to unload the ammunition from the MV 'Swat', were in the docks protecting the ammunition and the ship. The city of Chittagong itself was completely in the hands of the Awami League volunteers. Fortunately, nobody thought of distributing the twenty thousand rifles in the police lines meant for the Mujahids and Ansars.* The wing headquarters of the East Pakistan Rifles in Chittagong had decided to revolt. They were flying the Bangladesh flag atop their offices and had developed a strong defensive position which included dugouts and bunkers.

In view of this serious situation, I decided to return to Chittagong on 27 March and assume direct command. As I flew back in my helicopter, I instructed the pilot, Major (later Brigadier) Liaquat Israr Bukhari, to fly along the road to Comilla and look for Brigadier Iqbal Shafi's column. When we broke cloud cover and came low in a few moments, looking for the brigade column, we were greeted by a hail of machine-gun fire which hit the body of the aircraft. As a

---

* Police and Para-Military forces.

natural reaction, the pilot pulled the helicopter up into the clouds. I assessed the damage quickly. Our wireless system had been hit and put out of action, but the fuel tanks had a narrow escape. The second burst of bullets had hit the tailpipe but the control wires were intact. The crew and the passengers were fortunately unhurt, though a little shaken. Major Bukhari volunteered for another look at the area but I ruled it out as unnecessary and we proceeded back to Dhaka.

Next day, on 27 March, I sent a platoon of the 2 Commando Battalion for a surprise dawn raid on Chittagong airport. The action was a complete success. The rebels were caught unawares and the airport recaptured without the firing of a shot. The news was flashed back to me. Fortunately, we had one C-130 troop-carrier which we pressed into service. I flew in the first flight, along with my wireless detachment. Major General A.O. Mitha, together with Lieutenant Colonel Suleman and some officers and men of the 2 Commando Battalion, accompanied me on the first flight. They were to report to me at the Naval Headquarters in Chittagong, as I had decided to set up my command post there. In subsequent sorties, the aircraft was used to airlift a battalion of the Frontier Force.

After setting up my command post in the Naval Headquarters, Major General Mitha took charge of the commandos and launched them under Lieutenant Colonel Suleman. They were about a platoon strong, but some six officers accompanied Suleman on this mission. They were to advance along the main road and contact Brigadier Shafi's column, who had put up a successful attack on the rebel opposition and had advanced into the outskirts of Chittagong. Its

Commanding Officer, Lieutenant Colonel Shahpur, had been killed by a sniper's bullet in the initial stages. The column was now in regular wireless contact with my command set. The 20 Baluch Regiment was also in contact with me. However, they were halted by the 8 East Bengal Regiment who were putting up stout resistance.

As Lieutenant Colonel Suleman, who had served under me in the Pakistan Military Academy at Kakul, left at the head of his small mobile column, I stepped out to see him off. I had always held him in great esteem for his qualities as an officer and a gentleman. I was extremely unhappy at Mitha's decision to launch this small detachment of brave officers and men through the streets of a city that they did not know. They were accompanied by a young Bengali captain who had flown out from West Pakistan to check on the welfare of his family in Chittagong. Unfortunately, this contingent was ambushed and all the officers, excluding the Bengali captain, were killed. There were only three survivors, but when the bodies were recovered, the Bengali captain was not among those killed. He was mysteriously missing.

In subsequent flights on 27 March, the 25 Frontier Force Regiment was flown into Chittagong. I placed them under the personal command of Brigadier Ansari who knew Chittagong well. They were launched along the main road from the Naval Headquarters into the town. Brigadier Ansari's troops captured the radio station but that was of no great help. The transmitter was located on Kaptai Road, and Major Zia-ur-Rahman was making maximum use of the transmitter. He was inciting the Bengalis to rise in revolt, by putting out a lot of poisonous propaganda on the air. After the capture of the radio station, the rebel broadcasts did not cease. Consequently, I called for an air strike, which proved effective, and the station was put out of action. Before calling for the air strike, Mitha had launched the remnants of his commandos in boats, through the riverine route, with the mission to capture and destroy the transmitter. However, the commandos failed to reach their target. As in the previous fiasco, they were operating in unfamiliar terrain but this time they were cautious and did not suffer any casualties.

Brigadier Ansari, in the meantime, advanced to relieve the Naval Communication Centre at Tiger Pass and then proceeded to capture the Circuit House, the Railway Officers Colony, Deputy Commissioner's Hill, and Manora Hill. On 29 March, he captured the Reserve Police Lines along with the twenty thousand reserve rifles. Meanwhile, the 20 Baluch Regiment continued to exert pressure on the 8 East Bengal Regiment, who eventually disintegrated under pressure and fled along Kaptai Road to the hills.

On 29 March, the three columns linked up. The last rebel position to hold out was the headquarters of the East Pakistan Rifles. They had dug in defensive positions and were defiantly flying the Bangladesh flag. The position was attacked on 31 March under the command of Brigadier Shafi. To help him out, we gave him a troop of tanks that we had managed to activate. We also laid on gun support from the Pakistan Navy, as well as some infantry mortars. The attack went as planned and the rebels fled their positions. The Bangladesh flag was taken down and presented to me as a war trophy which I cherish to this day.

Leaving Brigadier Shafi in charge at Chittagong, I flew back to Dhaka on 1 April. I took Brigadier Ansari back with me to resume his duties as Commander of the Logistic Area. At Dhaka, I was put into the picture regarding the rest of the province. There was some unnecessary concern about the situation at Rangpur–Saidpur. The Governor and the Martial Law Administrator, Lieutenant General Tikka Khan, wanted me to proceed to Rangpur immediately, whereas I had just arrived from Chittagong after an absence of five days. I calmly had it conveyed to Tikka Khan that I was not to be treated as an errand boy, and that I would decide when and where to visit my command. I think he got the point for he sent Major General Mitha instead, to satisfy his curiosity. The latter brought back tidings of a favourable situation, which put his mind at rest. My thanks to Tikka Khan for avoiding a collision course and understanding an opposing point of view.

After the outbreak of hostilities in East Pakistan, I received numerous calls from West Pakistan seeking help for marooned relatives. Here, I will mention only two such personal appeals. Malik Sher Mohammad was my revered teacher and a close friend of my elder brother. I had enjoyed his personal hospitality, spending my summer vacation at his Soon Valley residence in village Padhrar in 1938. He had taken great pains to make my stay pleasant, so much so that even with the passage of over half a century I remember a lot of details with nostalgia. He rang me from Rawalpindi, barely audible. He informed me that his son-in-law, Major Mohammad Hussain, was in the East Pakistan Rifles at Thakurgaon in North Bengal. He was posted there, and was residing there with his wife and children when hostilities had already broken out. I spoke to Brigadier Abdullah Malik, at Rangpur, to rescue the family. When help reached the house, it was discovered that the whole family, including the Major, had been massacred by his own Bengali troops. One baby girl, however, had been saved by her Bengali *ayah** and handed over when help arrived.

The second instance was that of the late Colonel Dara's daughter. She was married to a young officer in the Civil Service of Pakistan. The young man was living with his wife at Tangail, some fifty miles north of Dhaka, on the road to Mymensingh. The outbreak of rebellion found them stranded at Tangail. The wife had the opportunity to return to safety in Dhaka, but she decided to stay with her husband through the crisis. A very worried uncle, Lieutenant General Riaz Hussain Shah, rang me from Quetta to help rescue the couple. They had been taken into custody by elements of the 2 East Bengal Regiment and were moved from place to place. Fortunately, their captors did not kill them. Later, when the relief column reached the Tangail area, the couple managed to escape and join the relief column. It was, indeed, a miraculous escape.

The recapture of Chittagong had broken the back of the rebels. They were on the run everywhere, trying to make for the nearest Indian territory. More troop reinforcements were arriving daily. The build-up of the 9 and 17 Divisions was progressing smoothly. Every day, we were getting news of our troops retaking important towns. As we could spare troops from Dhaka, we decided to launch 57 Brigade, under Brigadier Jahanzeb Arbab, into North Bengal. Brigadier Arbab and his brigade had performed excellently at Dhaka. He crossed the Padma River without opposition and captured

---
* A native nursemaid.

Pabna on the first day. From there, he captured Ishurdi and linked up with the Rajshahi garrison, pushing a column southwards to capture the all-important railway bridge over the Ganges at Paksey. Having achieved all these objectives in a whirlwind sweep, he turned north towards Bogra to link up with the 23 Brigade.

I paid a flying visit to Jessore where Brigadier Durrani had come under harsh criticism for being sluggish. My visit did him a lot of good. In the next few days, he affected a link-up with Khulna and advanced to the border post at Benapole. The intruding Indian Border Security Force came under harsh treatment and retreated in a hurry, leaving behind a few prisoners. Meanwhile, the 23 Brigade at Rangpur had fanned out and reported the capture of the towns of Mandalpara, Parbatipur and Nilfamari.

After my return from Chittagong on 1 April, I became very busy with operations in all the sectors of the province. Having pushed the rebels into full retreat all over the province, I thought it was a good psychological moment to announce an amnesty and tempt them to lay down their arms. If we failed to do so, the only alternative open to them would be to escape to the safe havens in India. The Indians would welcome them—to form the hardcore of a future army of resistance which, in due course, would re-enter East Pakistan as the vanguard of the Indian army. But I was afraid of Lieutenant General Tikka Khan's obstinacy. Earlier, when we had begun our military action, I had planned for Sheikh Mujib to be flown to Karachi, in secrecy, the same evening. Tikka Khan disagreed and said that he would publicly try Sheikh Mujib in Dhaka and hang him. The fallacy of his thinking soon became obvious. After first housing him in a girls' school, we had to shift him to the Command House. After a few days, though, he was secretly moved to West Pakistan. It was a relief for us to have him out of the way. Similarly, Tikka Khan ruled out an amnesty for the rebels. Needless to say, my worst fears came true in the months to come. The rebels formed the core of the Mukti Bahini* under Colonel M.A.G. Osmani.

Although Colonel Osmani had been superseded in promotion, strangely enough he became a permanent fixture in a very sensitive appointment at General Headquarters. He ran an open house at Rawalpindi for all Bengali officers in West Pakistan. His quarters at the Rawalpindi Club became a focal point for Bengali nationalism in the army. It was an open secret, known to all and sundry. However, Osmani continued with his parochial and nefarious activities, and those in authority did nothing to stop him. Ultimately, he emerged as Commander-in-Chief of the Mukti Bahini and played a significant role in the undoing of Pakistan.

My Bengali ADC, through no fault of his, had become redundant. He was a fine young man with deep Muslim League connections. He was the grandson of a prominent Muslim Leaguer, Maulana Akram Khan of Calcutta. He was married to the sister of Colonel Abdul Qayyum, who belonged to an elite family of Dhaka. At the start of his career, Qayyum had won both the Sword of Honour and the Norman Gold Medal for academics at the Pakistan Military Academy, Kakul. This was a rare distinction and has been repeated very infrequently in the fifty-year history of the

---
* Liberation Army.

Academy. I told Lieutenant Colonel (later Brigadier) Bashir Ahmed to speak to the Deputy Military Secretary and issue a posting order for my ADC. I nominated a suitable West Pakistani officer who was immediately available in Dhaka. The Deputy Military Secretary was surprised and, referring to me, retorted, 'Doesn't the General know that he is returning to West Pakistan? In fact, his relief is flying to Dhaka today and is already in the air.' When I returned to my headquarters, Lieutenant Colonel Bashir faced me, tears in his eyes and charged with emotion. He told me the news from General Headquarters and, somewhat reproachfully, said that I was leaving my boat in midstream and wondered what would become of the crew without their skipper. I had a very dedicated team at my headquarters, who were not only efficient but worked round the clock. The news came as a big shock. I felt as if the rug had been pulled from under my feet. I could not imagine that I could be moved without clearance from Lieutenant General Tikka Khan, who was my immediate superior. And I could think of no reason for Tikka Khan to agree to a replacement, at this critical juncture, when he was relying so heavily on me and I was delivering the goods to his entire satisfaction. After the first few days of adjustment, we had emerged as a well-knit team.

I felt deeply hurt and was fuming with anger until I clarified the situation with Lieutenant General Tikka Khan. We met at a scheduled conference at the headquarters of the Martial Law Administrator at 4 p.m. After the conference, I took Tikka Khan to his office to have a private word with him. I asked him why he had arranged my posting behind my back, without even saying a word to me about it beforehand. He was stupefied at the news. His immediate response was, 'Khadim, I swear to you on the Holy Quran that I had no prior knowledge and I am hearing the news from you for the first time. Lieutenant General Gul Hassan passed through this morning on his way to China, and even he did not mention [this].'

Tikka Khan's apologetic manner and concern somewhat pacified me. The same evening, we were flooded with the arrival of four general officers from West Pakistan. Major General A.A.K. Niazi had been promoted to Lieutenant General, and was to take over Eastern Command and Martial Law duties from Lieutenant General Tikka Khan. Major General Rahim Khan was to succeed me. Besides these, two senior officers, Major Generals Shaukat Riza and Nazar Hussain Shah arrived to takeover command of their respective Divisions, the bulk of which had already been flown into Dhaka. Incidentally, months later, when I asked Lieutenant General Gul Hassan about the circumstances of my posting from Dhaka, he too confirmed that he had no prior knowledge of it. Apparently, it was a decision confined to the President and the Chief of Army Staff. They are both dead and cannot answer the question. I can only guess that it was part of their strategy to induct 'hawks' of their choice, who might win a military victory for them in East Pakistan. To my mind, they were in a hopeless political and military situation. Defeat was inevitable unless they endeavoured to make peace with East Pakistan. The ego of the military dictator recoiled from taking such a course. Eventually, I reconciled myself to my transfer and was given command of the 7 Division with headquarters at Peshawar. It covered the whole of the North West Frontier Province. This position was a prestigious one for my rank. I recalled the prediction of Kala Chand at Dhaka. He had forecast that I would return to West

Pakistan before June 1971 with honour and dignity. Major General Rao Farman was stuck in Dhaka, and was to become a prisoner of war in December 1971. He came to see me off somewhat morosely. Kala Chand had predicted a long innings for him in the war-torn land.

Lieutenant General Niazi assumed the overall command on his arrival. I briefed Major General Rahim Khan with regard to the 14 Division's operational responsibilities and other relevant matters. I was to brief Niazi about the overall military situation in the province and give him suggestions on the conduct of operations in the foreseeable future on 11 March. I decided to depart from Dhaka on the first available flight, on 12 March. My wife and Mrs Farman had left for Karachi about four days earlier. My wife later told me that she stayed with Mrs Rahim Khan in Karachi. Until then, Rahim Khan had no idea of his posting to Dhaka. One morning, when they assembled for breakfast, Rahim started to criticize the senior commanders in Dhaka, especially me, although I happened to be a friend of his. He was of the opinion that the Bengalis were timid people and should have been subdued long ago. The reader can judge, for himself, the ignorance and lack of understanding of the East Pakistan situation among the hawks in the armed forces. My wife, however, quietly retorted that Rahim *Bhai** was totally ignorant about the situation in East Pakistan and would know it better if Allah sent him to Dhaka. Mrs Rahim was also upset at her husband's uncalled for remarks. In this sour atmosphere, created by Rahim's remark, my wife proceeded to the railway station to board her train for Lahore. The Rahims went to see her off. As the train started to pull out, and the Rahims were

---

* Brother.

waving goodbye, she saw the General's ADC rush towards them with a piece of paper which he handed to Major General Rahim Khan. At Hyderabad Railway Station, General Ihsan Malik had come to meet my wife and brought along some food. He confided to her that Major General Rahim Khan had been ordered to move to East Pakistan and relieve me. Allah has his own ways! Poor old Rahim had a rough time in East Pakistan. He was wounded and escaped with his life to Rangoon just before the surrender. The escape story became the subject of controversy later when the prisoners of war returned from India. Rahim was appointed Chief of the General Staff and was expected to succeed Lieutenant General Tikka Khan as Chief of the Army Staff. However, apparently, the return of the prisoners of war from India did not augur well for him. He was quietly retired from his job at the rank of Major General.

Let us return to Dhaka and pick up the threads of my narrative. On 10 April, I handed over charge of the 14 Division to Major General Rahim. I spent the rest of the day preparing briefing notes, on the conduct of future operations, for Lieutenant General Niazi. Tikka Khan used to hold a briefing/de-briefing conference in the Operations Room of the headquarters of the Eastern Command at 4 p.m. every evening. Till this day, all new arrivals had been placed under Command 14 Division. In other words, all operations were conducted through me. We assembled in the Operations Room at 4 p.m. as usual. The last to enter was Niazi, who was wearing a pistol holster on his webb belt. He announced that he had assumed command with immediate effect. He gave out some routine instructions for the future, including that all officers were to wear a pistol when in uniform. There was a sprinkling of Bengali officers in the gathering. To our consternation, Niazi became abusive and started raving. Breaking into Urdu, he said: '*Main is haramzadi qaum ki nasal badal doon ga. Yeh mujhe kiya samajhtey hain*'.* He threatened that he would let his soldiers loose on their womenfolk. There was pin-drop silence at these remarks. Officers looked at each other in silence, taken aback by his vulgarity. The meeting dispersed on this unhappy note with sullen faces. The next morning, we were given sad news. A Bengali officer, Major Mushtaq, who had served under me in Jessore, went into a bathroom at the Command Headquarters and shot himself in the head. He died instantaneously. A brilliant officer, he was dignified and self-respecting. I knew the officer well and his memory will always live with me. It is a pity that he should have been the first casualty of Niazi's words and deeds.

On the evening of 10 April 1971, the three newly-arrived general officers, except Lieutenant General Niazi, assembled at my residence. All three were good friends and known to me over a long period of time. They were poorly informed about the gravity of the situation in East Pakistan. Informally, I put them in the picture about the background and development of the current situation. When I finished, and before changing the subject, I jokingly made a remark about the bleak politico–military situation they faced. I wished them well, but expected to see them next when they would be repatriated to Pakistan via Wagah or Hussainiwala. Later, I cursed myself for making a cruel joke because, truly speaking, it was no joke but the pronouncement of a future reality. I don't think my friends took my remark seriously at

---
* They don't know me. I will change the race of this bastard nation.

the time, but I had an uncanny feeling that it would come true. They probably realized this months later when the noose tightened around them.

11 April was going to be my last day in Dhaka, as I had earlier handed over charge to Major General Rahim Khan. In the morning, I went over to Command Headquarters to meet Lieutenant General Niazi and discuss present and future operations with him. I had already asked him to have a map available in his office for discussion, but he had yet another surprise for me. In a very nonchalant manner, he put his hand on my shoulder and said: '*Yar, larai ki fikar nahin karo, woh to hum kar lain gey. Abhi to mujhey Bengali girlfriends kay phone number day do*'.* I knew Niazi fairly well, but was by no means on intimate terms with him. For a person of my disposition, these remarks were a thunderbolt. I could not imagine that any sane Pakistani could think in such terms in the midst of a civil war inflicted on the nation by its present rulers. With Niazi's words still ringing in my ears, I walked out saying, 'General, you should have known me better.' Leaving his office in disgust, I walked across to his Chief of Staff, Brigadier Ghulam Jilani Khan, with whom I left a piece of paper (Annexure C). I briefly discussed the contents with the Brigadier. I believe the deployment and conduct of operations, until 31 May 1971, broadly followed this pattern and was an unqualified success. What happened later is a matter of history. I left Dhaka, as planned, the next day— 12 April 1971—at 9 a.m. never to return again.

---

* Don't worry about the war my friend, we'll manage that. For now, just give me the phone numbers of your Bengali girlfriends.

9

Last Words . . .

My experience in East Pakistan, which covered a span of nearly two years, was very traumatic, to say the least. At very close quarters, I saw my beloved country broken up into two. It is quite incredible how lightly, portentous decisions were taken. Those at the top played with the destiny of the country in their personal quest for power. They did not seem moved by the massacre of the thousands of innocent men, women, and children. There was apparently one fixation in the minds of 'the trio'.

President Yahya Khan already held the reins of power and wanted to hold on to them by hook or by crook. Prior to the elections, his close aides and advisers had led him to believe that his position was invincible; they had calculated that, since no political party could win a decisive majority, the President would be in the position of an arbiter and would retain his position by playing one off against the other. On the other hand, Mujib had planned out his own strategy. He had a sprinkling of support in West Pakistan which he could depend on as it would always be there. He could count on dissidents like Wali Khan, Asghar Khan, Mian Mumtaz Daultana, G.M. Syed, and the like, but he planned to wipe out the opposition in East Pakistan. He used all the weapons in his political armoury to do that. He had plenty of time, too, to achieve it. He concentrated his time and propaganda overwhelmingly on East Pakistan, without bothering much about the Western wing. He targeted the '*shala* Punjabi' in every gathering and played on the sense of deprivation of the Bengalis.

One of Mujib's favourite targets was the Bihari community, which was invariably under fire and maligned for grabbing jobs which, he claimed, rightfully belonged to the Bengalis. He quoted mountains of statistics that were patently false. Bengal, which in my opinion was a bottomless well of problems, was depicted as the goose that laid the golden egg. He talked so often about *Sonar Bangla* that every Bengali came to believe it; even some West Pakistanis half-believed it. He managed to dupe Yahya Khan and his close advisers. Before the elections, he was always servile before the General and made all sorts of false promises that he never meant to fulfil. The President, somehow, failed to grasp that Sheikh Mujib committed himself unequivocally to the Six Points at every political meeting. How, then, could he go back on this oft-repeated commitment and compromise what he had preached for so long? It stood to reason that after his sweeping victory in the elections, Sheikh Mujib would become rigid about his political rights. It is strange that the President remained gullible, even after hearing the tape in which Sheikh Mujib had clearly spelt out his real intentions.

The third player of this 'trio', Bhutto, had worked hard in the pre-election period. He concentrated on only West Pakistan, and played upon the sentiments of the 'have nots'. His slogan of '*roti, kapra, aur makan*', which was very catchy and used in West Pakistan for the first time, appealed to a large number of people. However, he had little or no following in East Pakistan. By virtue of their political coverage and areas of operation, both leaders had a regional approach—an approach that was bound to encourage centrifugal tendencies. Bhutto's approach further encouraged a class-war between the 'haves' and the 'have nots' of society. These were dangerous developments and very evident to a serious observer during the latter half of 1970. The battle lines were drawn as soon as the results of the elections were known. Sheikh Mujib had a clear, overall majority and wanted all the power vested in himself and his party. He did not need a coalition and was not at all inclined to share power with Bhutto. On the other hand, Bhutto was not prepared to sit on the opposition benches. The situation was conspicuous by the lack of conciliation and accommodation for the other side. It is no wonder that the country slid into a situation of internecine struggle. To make matters worse, Yahya Khan decided to keep the two wings together through force of arms. The situation was further aggravated when India banned overflights, as a gesture of empathy for the East Pakistanis. In case of an outbreak of hostilities, the Pakistan Navy was in no position to keep 3000 miles of sea lines, between the two wings of Pakistan, open.

It is quite incredible that Yahya Khan chose the option of force. Any sane person could have seen the end result, and President Yahya Khan was no fool. In military circles, he had the reputation of possessing a sharp wit and a very penetrating and incisive mind. One can only guess at his motives because there is no available record of him revealing his thoughts to anyone. Some people are quick to say that he deliberately let go of East Pakistan, as he chose not to sit across the table to try and solve the problem through discussion; it had ramifications that no Federal Government could face and survive. Therefore, he let matters go the way they eventually did. This course was obviously very painful. A large number of families, particularly in the Punjab, saw their kith and kin in Indian prisoner of war camps. This widespread anguish had its own repercussions. There is another school of thought that believes that the President was slowly drugged by some of his female associates from East Pakistan. As a result, he became insensitive, indolent, and irresponsible. Whatever the reason, it does not mitigate the terrible tragedy that engulfed the entire Pakistani nation. Unfortunately, it also set a very bad precedent in national politics. During the last twenty years or so, we have been dealt one blow or another. During Bhutto's rule, there was the tribal uprising in Balochistan, when the leadership used repression and forced the dissident leaders to flee the country. The latter's nefarious designs of returning with Russian tanks were also defeated.

In Afghanistan, the Russian monolith was defeated by the Mujahideen in an unprecedented feat of arms. Communism received a mortal blow. The Soviet Union disintegrated and, with it, the Soviet satellites went helter-skelter. Pakistan, too, has been facing many adversities. However, given the honesty of purpose and the will to surmount our difficulties, I have no doubt that the Pakistani nation will emerge united and stronger than ever before. Nevertheless, the Pakistan nation must analyse the tragedy of East Pakistan in detail, recognize the mistakes made, and resolve not to repeat them. In the ensuing paragraphs, I will place, before the reader, what I consider is the moral of my story.

The British replaced the Muslim power in India. The advent of the British began in Calcutta and expanded westwards. With the defeat of Nawab Sirajuddaulah at the Battle of Plassey in 1757, the Muslims were crushed and reduced to the level of serfs and menials. The British created a class of Hindu rajas and landlords in Bengal who dominated and exploited the Muslim peasantry. The British also created a class of clerks and petty officials from the Hindu polity, who formed the hard-core of British administration and wielded a great deal of power. This situation posed a challenge to the Muslims in East India. It is, therefore, small wonder that the All-India Muslim League was born in Dhaka in 1906. And, when the time came for the Indian movement for independence, the Muslims of Bengal were at the forefront, agitating against Hindu domination and demanding a separate homeland for themselves. Maulvi Fazlul Haque from East Bengal pioneered the Pakistan Resolution in Lahore in March 1940. The Resolution was rather ambiguous and did not categorically ask for two separate homelands for the Muslims, one in the west and another in the east. In this ambiguous situation, no one set up a committee or commission to study the problems of running a federated state in such a situation. Thus, we plunged headlong into a united Pakistan. As the initial euphoria wore off, we started to realize the problems of running a federation a thousand miles apart. As luck would have it, Quaid-i-Azam Mohammad Ali Jinnah, the Father of the Nation, left us after only a year, followed by Liaquat Ali Khan, the first Prime Minister of Pakistan, who was assassinated in 1951. Others who followed did not prove equal to the task. We had hardly come into being as a country when the process of disintegration set in.

The religion of Islam was a common bond between the people of both wings. However, it could not make up for the shortcomings caused by physical separation and by the differences in language and culture. The large Hindu minority—about 17 per cent in East Pakistan—took advantage of these differences and did all they could to emphasize and accentuate them. The Urdu language was the first issue to come under attack. The Bengalis refused to look upon it as the official and national language of the country. Thus, with one stroke, the Bengali Muslims were divided from the West Pakistanis, and even from the Bihari settlers in East Pakistan. The Bihari settlers remain divided, to date, from the rest of the Bengalis, and are in a miserable state.[1] They have not been provided opportunities to assimilate with the inhabitants of the land of their choice. They have been singled out and condemned to live as refugees in what was the Eastern wing of Pakistan. The Bengali Hindus became one with the Bengali Muslims, through the medium of the Bengali language and the so-called Bengali culture. In the Bengali culture, there is a lot of emphasis on music and dancing by both sexes, while the maulanas of the Western wing had a puritanical approach, which has become more and more uncompromising with the passage of time.

Developments in the last twenty years have been rather significant. A military dictator of long-standing was overthrown in the agitation pioneered by two ladies (Sheikh Hasina and Khaleda Zia) in Bangladesh. One of them captured power through the ballot and currently heads the government.[2] In Pakistan, a woman (Benazir Bhutto) came to power through the ballot after the demise of a military dictator (Ziaul Haq) in 1988. However, she could not survive long as head of the government. Her government was prematurely dismissed. In the new elections, she had to be satisfied with the position of the Leader of the Opposition. So much for democracy in Bangladesh and Pakistan.

Economic factors also played a significant role in the undoing of Pakistan. East Pakistan had a total land area of some 55,000 square miles, the bulk of which was a flat plain with an intricate network of rivers. The province was susceptible to annual flooding during the monsoons because of heavy rains and poor drainage. Three paddy harvests were possible during the year but because of the lack of winter rains and no means of artificial irrigation, perforce the major paddy crop was during the monsoon. This crop was invariably severely damaged by the annual flooding. The people of East Pakistan were basically rice-eaters—and averse to the consumption of wheat as part of their diet—of which there was always a shortage. This difficult situation was further compounded by a very high density of population.

East Pakistan had less than one-fifth of the land area of West Pakistan, but its population was 54 per cent of the total national population. Undoubtedly, there were areas of poverty and economic deprivation in West Pakistan too. For example, much of Balochistan is poor and backward. But, the poverty I saw in the rural areas of East Pakistan was unmatched in West Pakistan. Most of the people in the villages looked starved and famished. To make matters worse, they were either indolent or unemployed. Land-holdings were generally so small that even bullock cultivation, let alone mechanized cultivation, was not possible. In this environment, there was an acute sense of economic deprivation. By

Bidding farewell to HQ 107 BDE

Seeing off the outgoing General Officer Commanding (GOC), 14 Division Major General Muzaffaruddin (left, in civilian clothes).

President Yahya Khan on one of his visits to Dhaka.

Observing a march past with Lieutenant General Sahibzada Yaqub Khan, 31 December 1969.

With Lieutenant General Sahibzada Yaqub Khan and COAS General Abdul Hamid. Officers' Mess, Dhaka.

With Lieutenant General M. Attiqur Rahman.

With Major General Rao Farman Ali.

With officers and JCOs.

At the Division Sports.

At a military exercise with COAS Abdul Hamid Khan and Company Commandant 29 Cavalry Lt. Col. Sagheer Hussain Syed (later Lieutenant General).

With officers of the 29 Cavalry, Rangpur.

At the Narayanganj Rifle Club

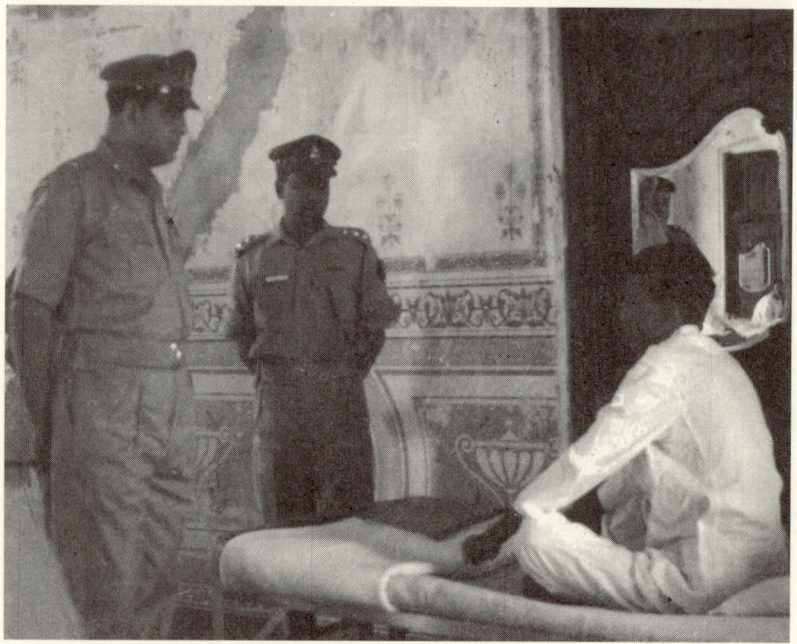

First visit to 10 Field Ambulance, Rangpur, East Pakistan, 29 November 1969

Field visit with the COAS General Abdul Hamid Khan.

Inspecting the Information Room on a visit to 3 CDO BN (SSG).

With wife Rafia.

With father-in-law Malik Sardar Khan Noon at a meena bazaar in Dhaka.

Field Marshal Mohammad Ayub Khan

General A.M. Yahya Khan

General Abdul Hamid Khan

Lt. Gen. S.G.M.M. Peerzada

Lt. Gen. Tikka Khan

Lt. Gen. Amir Abdullah Khan Niazi

Maj. Gen. Rao Farman Ali

Vice-Admiral S.M. Ahsan

Zulfikar Ali Bhutto

Sheikh Mujibur Rahman

temperament, the people were very volatile and easily excitable. Like most illiterate people, they were also very gullible. If you sneezed loudly enough on the streets of Dhaka or any other large town, you could collect a crowd of several thousands in a few minutes! I was once flying over North Bengal. For some reason, my helicopter touched down at an unknown place for a few minutes. In that comparatively sparsely populated area, we drew a crowd of several thousand in a few minutes. People seemed to appear from nowhere like ants. I think I have adequately emphasized the overpopulation, lack of flood protection, and lack of initiative among the people.

At the time of Independence in 1947, East Pakistan did not have any industry worth its name. It merely formed the hinterland for the jute industry in Calcutta. Independence offered attractive opportunities for setting up industries based on local raw materials. The indigenous people did not have the capital and also lacked the initiative and know-how. Most entrepreneurs were non-Bengalis, like the Ispahanis, Adamjees, and Bawanys. The number of Bengali families owning any sizeable industry could be counted on the fingers of one hand. By contrast, growth of industry in West Pakistan, particularly in Karachi, was explosive. This further added to the disparity between the two wings and contributed to the widening gulf.

There were also many administrative anomalies. East Pakistan did not have a military tradition. There were very few officers and men in the armed forces. We could have taken great strides in the induction of Bengalis in the span of some twenty years. Unfortunately, this was not done. The armed forces largely remained the preserve of West Pakistan. One could say the same about the civil service, over twenty years after Independence. The Federal Government continued to perpetrate this imbalance. To quote a specific example of the imbalance, a Punjabi youth who was 11th in the order of merit in a Central Superior Services Examination was dropped from the District Management Group whereas a Bengali counterpart who was 180th was accepted to make up the 50 per cent quota for the Bengalis. Obviously, such glaring disparities could not lead to a uniformly efficient service. The Bengalis lagged far behind in the services. As a result of this disparity, East Pakistani officials saw a bright future and rapid promotion for themselves in an independent Bangladesh. The historic example of the independent state of Pakistan was too recent to be forgotten. Young officials were then catapulted into positions of great responsibility. Thus, the young East Pakistani officials became a strong vested interest group which looked forward to the emergence of an independent and sovereign state of Bangladesh.

While examining the situation in the services, I would like to mention one other important aspect. The senior civil servants from West Pakistan who went to serve in East Pakistan adopted a haughty, colonial attitude towards the public in East Pakistan. They considered themselves the successors of the British rulers and, instead of seeing their mission as one of serving the people, adopted superior airs. This attitude deeply hurt the egos of the educated and politically oriented Bengalis. The cauldron started to bubble in this environment, waiting to overflow at an opportune moment.

At the time of independence, Karachi was designated as the seat of government. Soon, the government began to get organized. New departments and institutions began to take shape. No consideration was given to our peculiar geographical situation and the inter-wing distances. All controlling headquarters were located in Karachi. Later, the capital was shifted to Islamabad. It was a good decision but it added to the inter-wing distance. Field Marshal Ayub Khan showed some vision and started to plan and construct a second capital at Dhaka. However, this was not a high priority on the development agenda. Having been allocated meagre resources, the project had shown little progress by the time of East Pakistan's secession. A strong centre had evolved, where all the power was vested. One had to make several trips to Karachi, from anywhere in Pakistan, to get anything done, whether it was sanction for an industry or a loan to set it up. It was obviously very tiresome and expensive for the Bengalis to make repeated trips to Karachi. They would rather have travelled the much shorter distance, from Chittagong, Khulna, or Rajshahi, to Dhaka. Nothing was done to correct this unhappy situation and, if anything was done, it was belated and too little. Towards the tail-end, the head office of the Industrial Development Bank was shifted to Dhaka. A cousin of my wife's who, at that time, was involved in setting up a textile mill, paid only two visits to Dhaka. Although he had the convenience of my presence and related facilities there, at the end of his second visit, even though his work was completed, he complained of the inconvenience of travelling to Dhaka. This factor was not the last straw, but it certainly was a considerable irritant.

Then there was the important factor of a strong Hindu minority of 17 per cent in East Pakistan, and the irreconcilable and hostile attitude of India towards the birth of the Muslim state of Pakistan. The Congress leaders of India could not stop the birth of an Islamic state to both the north-east and the north-west of India. But, they started to work against it, to undo this fledgling country from the day of its inception. East Pakistan was chosen as the most susceptible target and every effort was made to undermine its unity with the rest of the country. There are numerous stories to illustrate this point. We allowed the enemy to succeed and proved unable to safeguard our hard-won independence. We must accept the blame for this, fairly and squarely. But the story does not end there. The enemy has not given up. He is now trying to break up the remnants of Pakistan. We must recognize the threat and revitalize our will to live as an independent and self-respecting people. We must make Pakistan strong enough to repel any aggression from outside, and thwart any designs of subversion from within. I have no prescription or panacea to offer but I have some thoughts for the consideration of my people.

Pakistan was created as a homeland for the Muslims of the subcontinent and not for any particular class of Muslims. Millions of people left their homes and hearths, and went through untold suffering, to reach its borders for safety. We, therefore, created a country worth fighting and dying for. Let us keep it that way. We are the custodians of a glorious tradition. Let our future generations remember us with good words. Every Pakistani must feel that he has a stake in this country and should gladly offer any sacrifice to safeguard its honour and integrity. Let us live by a code of ethics in which loyalty to the country comes first and foremost—above all other tribal and ethnic loyalties. We are Pakistanis first and foremost. Everything else comes afterwards.

Pakistan *Paindabad*!*

Notes

1. Some 150,000 Urdu-speaking Muslim refugees have the right to be Bangladesh citizens, a court has ruled. The Dhaka High Court ruling applies to those who were minors when Bangladesh won independence in 1971 or born after. The Biharis, as they are known locally, moved from India to what was then East Pakistan following partition in 1947. The high court said refugees who were minors at the time of Bangladesh's war of independence in 1971 and those who were born after would also gain the right to vote. The judgement does not cover refugees who were adults at the time of independence. 'Citizenship for Bihari refugees', BBC News, 2008-05-19, 7407757, http://news.bbc.co.uk/go/pr/fr/-/2/hi/south_asia/7407757.stm. Retrieved 2008-05-21.
2. Sheikh Hasina is the eldest of the five children of Sheikh Mujibur Rahman. She was the Prime Minister of Bangladesh from 23 June 1996 to 15 July 2001. She again assumed the office of the Prime Minister in June 2009.

---

* Persian word meaning long live.

Annexure A

Extract of Article by Rehman Sobhan, *South Asian Review*, London, July 1971

Yakub's replacement was backed up by a continuous inflow of reinforcements for the garrisons. Yahya in a speech on March 6 had given further provocation by blaming Mujib for the crisis and not even alluding to Bhutto. His offer to reconvene the Assembly on March 25 was seen as belated and inadequate and as having been put in a context in which it was rendered virtually irrelevant. For this reason it was believed by many that Mujib would use his public meeting of March 7 to proclaim independence, since Yahya had shown no willingness to come to terms with the consequences of his earlier decision. The army itself was put on full alert to go into action on March 7 in the event of such a declaration.

Mujib realised that any such proclamation would invoke massive carnage on Bengalis, and was reluctant to assume such a responsibility. His decision to persevere with non-cooperation while leaving the door open for a negotiated settlement within Pakistan was a compromise between the counter-pressures of the street and Army. There is no doubt that between March 1 and 7 he was under intense pressure to proclaim independence, and this became greater still after Yahya's broadcast on March 6. But by the afternoon of March 7 he had successfully contained these pressures and committed his party to negotiations within the framework of Pakistan. Subsequent suggestions that he lost control to extremist elements in his party bear no relation to the facts, and overlook the point that the crucial issue had been resolved before March 7, after which Mujib's authority on all substantive issues was unchallenged within the party. When, for instance, student leaders decided unilaterally to impose a customs check on West Pakistanis leaving Dacca, it took Mujib precisely four hours to get this withdrawn. It was largely the unchallenged nature of his authority which enabled him to use his volunteers to preserve law and order throughout the province during this period. Given the charged atmosphere, this was no mean achievement. It can be confirmed by a host of foreign journalists who had congregated in Dacca hoping to witness a major convulsion.

Rehman Sobhan is a prominent Bangladeshi economist and civil society leader. He played a leading role in the Bengali nationalist movement in the 1960s, including authoring the Two Economies Theory and drafting the Six-point demands of Sheikh Mujibur Rahman. He also served in the first Planning Commission in Bangladesh. Presently, Rehman Sobhan heads the Centre for Policy Dialogue (CPD), Bangladesh's leading public policy think-tank.

Annexure B
Operational Details of 'Operation Searchlight'

Basis for Planning

1. AL [Awami League] action and reactions to be treated as rebellion and those who support or defy ML [Martial Law] action be dealt with as hostile elements.
2. As AL has widespread support even amongst the EP [East Pakistani] elements in the Army the operation has to be launched with great cunningness, surprise, deception and speed combined with shock action.

Basic Requirements for Success

3. The operation to be launched all over the Province simultaneously.
4. Maximum number of political and student leaders and extremists amongst teaching staffs, cultural organizations to be arrested. In the initial phase top political leaders and top student leaders must be arrested.
5. Operation must achieve a hundred per cent success in Dacca. For that Dacca University will have to be occupied and searched.
6. Security of cantonments must be ensured. Greater and freer use of fire against those who dare attack the cantonment.
7. All means of internal and international communications to be cut off. Telephone exchanges, Radio, TV, Teleprinter services, transmitters with foreign consulates to be closed down.
8. EP tps [troops] to be neutralized by controlling and guarding kotes and ammunition by WP [West Pakistani] tps. Same for PAF and EPR.

Surprise and Deception

9. **At higher plane:** it is requested that the President may consider the desirability of continuing the dialogue—even of deceiving Mujib that

ANNEXURE B

even though Mr Bhutto may not agree, he will make an announcement on 25 March conceding to the demands of AL etc.

10. **At Tactical Level**

    a. As secrecy is of paramount importance, preliminary operations given below should be carried out by tps already located in the city:

        (1) Breaking into Mujib's house and arresting all present. The house is well-guarded and well-defended.
        (2) Surrounding the important halls of the Universities—Iqbal Hall DU [Dacca University], Jagan Nath Hall, Liaqat Hall Engineering University.
        (3) Switching off telephone exchange.
        (4) Isolating known houses where weapons etc. have been collected.

    b. No activity by tps in the cantonment area till telephone exchange has been switched off.
    c. Nobody should be allowed to go out of the cantonment after 2200 hrs on the night of operation.
    d. On one excuse or the other tps in the city should be reinforced in the area of the President's House, Governor's House, MNA Hostel, Radio, TV and Telephone exchange premises.
    e. Civilian cars may have to be used for operation against Mujib's house.

Sequence of Actions

11. a. H Hr—0100 hrs.
    b. **Timings for Move Out**

        (1) Commando [one Platoon]—Mujib's House—0100 hrs.
        (2) Telephone exchange switched off—2455 hrs.
        (3) Tps earmarked for cordon Universities—0105 hrs.
        (4) Tps from the city to Rajarbagh Police HQ and other PS [Police station] nearby—0105 hrs.
        (5) Following places surrounded—0105 hrs:

(a) Mrs Anwara Begum's House, Rd No. 29.
(b) House No. 148, Rd No. 29.

(6) Curfew imposed—0110 hrs by Siren (arrange) by loudspeakers. Duration 30 hrs initially. No passes for the initial phase. Due consideration to be given only to cases of delivery and serious heart attack etc. Evac by Army on request. Also announce that there will be no newspapers brought out till further orders.

(7) Tps move out to respective sectors with specific missions—0110 hrs. (For tp alert a drill to be evolved). Halls occupied and searched.

(8) Tps move to University area—0500 hrs.

(9) Rd blocks and riverine block estb—0200 hrs.

c. **Operations during the Day Time**

(1) House to house search of Dhanmandi suspected houses, also Hindu houses in old city (int to collect data).

(2) All printing presses to be closed down. All cyclostyling machines in the University, Colleges (T&T) and Physical Training Institute and Technical Institute to be confiscated.

(3) Curfew imposed with severity.

(4) Other leaders arrested.

12. **Allotment of Tps to Tasks.** Details to be worked out by B[riga]de Com[man]d[er] but the following must be done:

a. Kotes of EP units taken over, including Sig[nal]s and other administrative units. Arms to be given only to WP personnel. Explanation: We did not wish to embarrass the EP tps and did not want them to be used in tasks which may not be pleasant to them.

b. Police stations to be disarmed.

c. DG [Director General] EPR [East Pakistan Rifles] to ensure security of his kotes.

d. All Ansar Rifles to be got hold of.

ANNEXURE B

13. **Info Required**
    a. Whereabouts of the following:
        (1)   Mujib
        (2)   Nazarul Islam
        (3)   Tajuddin
        (4)   Osmani
        (5)   Sirajul Alam
        (6)   Mannan
        (7)   Ataur Rahman
        (8)   Professor Muzaffar
        (9)   Oli Ahad
        (10) Mrs Motia Chaudhry
        (11) Barrister Maudud
        (12) Faizul Haq
        (13) Tofail
        (14) Nure Alam Siddiqui ⎫
        (15) Rauf   ⎬ and other student leaders.
        (16) Makhan   ⎭

    b. Location of all police stations and of Rifles.
    c. Location of strong points and arsenal houses in the city.
    d. Location of tr[ainin]g camps and areas etc.
    e. Location of Cultural Centres which are being used for imparting military trg.
    f. Names of ex-service officers who are actively helping insurrectional movement.

14. **Command and Control.** Two commands be established:

    a. **Dacca Area**
        Comd — Major General Farman
        Staff — Eastern Comd Staff/or HQ ML
        Tps — Loc[ated] in Dacca.

b. **The Rest of the Province**

    Comd — Major General K.H. Raja
    Staff — HQ 14 Div
    Tps — Less those in Dacca

15. **Security of the Cantonment**

    a. **Phase I** De-escalate. All arms including PAF deposited.

16. **Communication**

    a. Security.
    b. Layout.

ALLOTMENT OF TROOPS TO TASKS

Dacca

Command and Control: Maj. Gen. Farman with HQ MLA Zone B.

Troops

HQ 57 Brigade with troops in Dacca, i.e. 18 Punjab, 32 Punjab (CO to be replaced by [Lt. Col.] Taj, GSO I [Int]), 22 Baluch, 13 Frontier Force, 31 Field Regt., 13 Light Ack-Ack Regt., company of 3 Commando (from Comilla).

Tasks

a. Neutralize by disarming 2 and 10 East Bengal, HQ East Pakistan Rifles (2500), Reserve Police at Rajar Bagh (2000).
b. Exchange and transmitters, Radio, TV, State Bank.
c. Arrest Awami League leaders—detailed lists and addresses.
d. University Halls, Iqbal, Jagan Nath, Liaqat (Engineering University).
e. Seal off town including road, rail and river. Patrol river.
f. Protect factories at Ghazipur and Ammo Depot at Rajendrapur.

Remainder: Under Maj. Gen. K.H. Raja and HQ 14 Div.

Jessore

Troops

HQ 107 Brigade, 25 Baluch, 27 Baluch, Elements of 24 Field Regt., 55 Field Regt.

Tasks

a. Disarm 1 East Bengal and Sector HQ East Pakistan Rifles and Reserve Police incl. Ansar weapons.
b. Secure Jessore town and arrest Awami League and student leaders.
c. Exchange and telephone communications.
d. Zone of security round cantt., Jessore town and Jessore–Khulna road, airfield.
e. Exchange at Kushtia to be made inoperative.
f. Reinforce Khulna if required.

Khulna

Troops

22 FF

Tasks

a. Security in town.
b. Exchange and Radio Station.
c. Wing HQ East Pakistan Rifles, Reserve Companies and Reserve Police to be disarmed.
d. Arrest Awami League students and communist leaders.

Rangpur–Saidpur

Troops

HQ 23 Brigade, 29 Cavalry, 26 Frontier Force, 23 Field Regt.

Tasks

a. Security of Rangpur–Saidpur.

b. Disarm 3 East Bengal at Saidpur.
c. If possible disarm Sector HQ and Reserve Company at Dinajpur or neutralize by dispersal Reserve Company by reinforcing border outposts.
d. Radio Station and telephone exchange at Rangpur.
e. Awami League and student leaders at Rangpur.
f. Ammo dump at Bogra.

Rajshahi

Troops

25 Punjab

Tasks

a. Despatch CO—Shafqat Baluch.
b. Exchange and Radio Station Rajshahi.
c. Disarm Reserve Police and Sector HQ East Pakistan Rifles.
d. Rajshahi University and in particular Medical College.
e. Awami League and student leaders.

Comilla

Troops

53 Field Regt., 1½ Mortar Batteries, Station troops, 3 Commando Batallion (less Company)

Tasks

a. Disarm 4 EB, Wing HQ East Pakistan Rifles, Reserve District Police.
b. Secure town and arrest Awami League leaders and students.
c. Exchange.

ANNEXURE B

SYLHET

Troops

31 Punjab less company

Tasks

a. Radio Station, Exchange.
b. Keane Bridge over Surma
c. Airfield.
d. Awami League and student leaders.
e. Disarm Section HQ East Pakistan Rifles and Reserve Police. Liaison with Sikandar.

CHITTAGONG

Troops

20 Baluch, less advance party; company 31 Punjab present ex Sylhet; Iqbal Shafi to lead a mobile column from Comilla by road and reinforce S.T. 0100 hrs (H hrs) on D-day.

Mobile Column: Brig. Iqbal Shafi with Tac HQ and Communications; 24 Frontier Force; Troop Heavy Mortars; Field Company Engineers; Company in advance to Feni on evening D-day.

Tasks

a. Disarm EBRC, 8 East Bengal, Section HQ East Pakistan Rifles, Reserve Police.
b. Seize Central Police Armoury (Twenty thousand Ansar rifles).
c. Radio Station and Exchange.
d. Liaise with Pakistan Navy (Commodore Mumtaz).
e. Liaise with Shigri and Janjua (CO 8 East Bengal) who have been instructed to take orders from you till arrival Iqbal Shafi.
f. If Shigri and Janjua feel sure about their outfits then do not disarm. In that case merely put in a road block to town from Cantt. by placing a company in defensive position so that later EBRC and 8 East Bengal Rifles are blocked should they change their loyalties.

g. I am taking Brig. Mozamdar with me. Arrest Chaudhary (CI EBRC) on D-day night.
h. Arrest of Awami League and student leaders after above accomplished.

Annexure C
Recommendations Regarding Military Operations, 11 April 1971

1. Mil ops to finish before monsoon i.e. 15 May. Grace period of another 15 days. Monsoon break 1 June 71.

2. **Priorities**
   a. Seal main routes from Indian Border.
   b. Open main routes of comm—own.
   c. Take main towns.
   d. Visit other towns.

3. **Assessment of Tasks**

   Rajshahi Division (16 Div)

   a. Bn — North of Teasta incl L. Hat)
   b. Bn — Rangpur   )
   c. Bn — Saidpur   ) One Bde
   d. Bn — Thakargaon   ) Rangpur
   (One Arty Reg., One R & S Bn and one Armd Regt)
   e. Bn — Rajshahi   )
   f. Bn — Ishurdi   )
   g. Bn — Pabna   ) One Bde Natore
   h. Bde HQ Natore   )
   j. Arty— Fd Reg   )
   k. Bn — Bogra   )
   l. Bn — Noagaon   ) Div HQ, One Bde & Armd Regt
   m. Bde HQ Bogra   )
   n. Div HQ Bogra   )

Total Tps

Div HQ, three Bde HQ, 9 Inf Bns, Armd Regt, Two Fd Regts, one R&S Bn (could economize one inf bn)

Dacca and Khulna Division (14 Div Area)

    a.   Khulna—Dacca Civ Divisions.
    b.   Problem of open border in Jessore.

Jessore

a.	Bn	–	Khulna incl Satkhira
b.	Bn	–	Jessore
c.	R&S Bn	–	Jessore
d.	Bde HQ	–	Jessore
e.	Bn	–	Khushtia and Mor Bty
f.	Bn	–	Barisal–Patuakhali (Later to be visited through River route)
g.	Bn	–	Faridpur
h.	Bde HQ	–	Faridpur

Total Tps

Two Bde HQ, five bns, R&S, one fd regt and one mor bty.

Dacca

a.	One Bde of three Bns—Dacca City and Cantt.
b.	Bde HQ	–	Joydebpur
c.	Bn	–	Joydebpur
d.	Bn	–	Mymensingh
e.	Fd Regt	–	Dacca

Total Tps

Div HQ, Two Bde HQ, five bns and one fd regt.

ANNEXURE C

Chittagong Divison (9 Div Area)

    a. Sylhet   –   One Bde HQ, three Bns, Mor Bty.
    b. Comilla   –   Div HQ, Bde HQ, three Bns, One Fd Regt.
    c. Chittagong –   Bde HQ, four Bns, Mor Bty.

Grand Total

	Div HQ	Bde HQ	Cav Regt	Inf Bn	R&S	Fd Regt	Mor Bty
	1 (Bogra)	3	1	9	1	2	1
	1 (Dacca)	4	–	10	1	2	1
	1 (Comilla)	3	–	10	–	1	2
	3	10	1	29	2	5	4
Present	3	9	1	23	2	4	2
Shortages	–	1	–	6	–	1	2

    a. Could possibly economize on one bn.
    b. Engr units (RSU, Navy, Rly Bn, Port Bn).
    c. Army Avn (Helicopters, a few fixed wing).
    d. PAF (Tpt ac)

4. **Development of Ops**

Rajshahi Division

    a. 23 Bde—Capture Dinajpur and develop ops to the North–Thakargaon–Pachagarh.
    b. 57 Bde—Complete present op and develop op to Bogra along road.
    c. New Bde—To be built up in Rangpur–Isherdi and op to Bogra and seal Hilly.

Jessore

    a. Give them one more Bn.
    b. Capture area Chaudange–Meherpur–Kushtia and link up with 57 Bde at Paksey.
    c. Later one bn to visit Barisal–Patua by river route.
    d. Later one bn to visit Faridpur by rd.
    e. Addl coy to Khulna. Take Sitkhira and seal border as pri.

Comilla Sec
- a. One more bn to Sylhet and drive South on B Baria.
- b. Comilla grn North to B Baria.
- c. Comilla grn South to Feni and Beyond.
- d. Chittagong grn at present seal Karnafuli and drive North to Feni to link up with c above.

Dacca
- a. Bhairab
- b. Memonsingh–Jamalpur–Netra Kona–Kishore Ganj.

Index

A

Adamjee College, 55
Adamjees, 55, 107
Afghanistan, 103
Agartala, 84; Conspiracy Case, 13, 27 n.1; conspirators, 23
Ahmed, Lt. Col. Bashir, 94
Ahmed, Lt. Col. Riaz, 22, 25
Ahmed, Maulvi Farid, 28
Ahsan, Admiral Syed Mohammad, xvi, 18, 23, 43, 48, 54, 56, 70
All-India Muslim League, 104
Amin, Nurul, 28, 34
Anis-uz-Zaman, 37
Ansari, Brigadier Mohammad Hussain, 18, 66, 74, 75, 88, 89, 90
Arbab, Brigadier Jahanzeb, 27, 71, 90
Army War Course, 1–3, 5, 6
Artillery 2 Corps, 7, 9
Asghar, Brigadier Mohammad, 3
Awami League, xvii, xix, 11, 15, 22, 29, 30, 33, 34, 39, 40, 44 n.1, 47, 48, 57, 59, 74; candidates, 34; extremists in, 59, 60; high command, 51; hooligan elements, 17, 28; leaders, 32, 79; leadership, 14, 39; members, 41, 54; militants, 10; ruffians, 29, 33; student leaders, 60; volunteers, 60, 72, 86; workers, 49, 60; Working Committee, 49, 59, 60
Azam, Ghulam, 29

B

Babar, Lt. Col. Naseerullah Khan, 27, 38
Baghdad, 8
Balochistan, 44 n.1, 103, 106
Baluch Regiment, 11, 74, 88, 89
Baluch, Lt. Col. Shafqat, 76, 83
Bangladesh, xiii, xiv, 14, 33, 35, 53, 76, 84, 86, 89, 105, 106, 108
Barisal, 38, 43
Battle of Plassey, 104
Benapole, 43, 83, 92
Bengali(s), 5, 6, 10, 14, 15, 17, 21, 33, 43, 60, 63, 66, 71, 80, 84, 85, 88, 99, 101, 105, 107–109; army, 24; bureaucrats, 37; community, 54; infantry battalions, 25; language, 6, 105; officer(s), 11, 24, 26, 74, 93, 98; population, xix; press, 38; troops, 13, 23, 24, 51, 67–69, 76, 79, 83, 91; women, xvii
Bhashani, Maulana, 21, 29
Bhutto, Benazir, 105
Bhutto, Zulfikar Ali, xviii, xix, 4, 39–41, 48, 63, 71, 72, 101–103
Bihari(s), 5, 6, 10, 16, 17, 53, 69, 101, 105, 111
Bogra, 43, 92
Brahmanbaria, 43, 84
British, 3, 24, 38, 104, 108
Bukhari, Major Liaquat Israr, 86, 87

C

Chaudhary, Lt. Col., 85
Chaudhry, Fazlul Qader, 28

Chittagong Hill Tracts, 34
Choudhury, G.W., 30
Chuadanga, 77, 82
Comilla, 68, 73, 75, 76, 78, 81, 84, 86
Calcutta, 10, 46, 51, 61, 93, 104, 107
Central Government, xx, 10, 11, 14, 15, 22, 32, 33, 38, 49
Chittagong, 16, 25, 34, 36, 68, 73–76, 78, 79, 81, 85–88, 90–92, 109

D

Dara, Colonel, 91
Darsana, 43
Dastagir, Lt. Col. Golam, 11
Daultana, Mian Mumtaz, 100
Dhaka Garrison, 23, 71
Dhaka Television Station, 67
Dhaka University, 18, 46, 54, 79, 81
Dhaka, 5, 9, 13–19, 21–23, 25, 27, 29, 34, 36–38, 41, 42, 46, 48, 49, 51–57, 62–65, 67, 68, 71–73, 75, 76, 78–82, 84, 87, 90–97, 99, 104, 107, 109
Dhanmandi, 51, 60
Durbar Hall, 17
Durrani, Brigadier, 76, 92

E

East Bengal Battalion, 25, 26, 78
East Bengal Regimental Centre, 18, 73, 74, 76, 85
East Pakistan Logistic Area, 18
Election Commission, 32, 34
El-Edroos, Brigadier Ali, 52, 76
Eleven-Point Programme, 41
East Pakistan Rifles, 16, 17, 79, 82, 86, 89, 90
East Pakistani(s), 5, 6, 14, 17, 33, 38, 54, 61, 67, 84, 102, 108
East Pakistan, 5, 6, 9, 11, 13, 14, 16–18, 20–28, 30–34, 36, 38, 40, 43, 46–49, 52–54, 57–59, 61, 63, 64, 66, 67, 70, 74, 78, 79, 90, 92, 95–98, 100–103, 105–110
East Bengal Regiment, 11, 18, 26, 68, 75, 78, 82, 84, 88, 89, 91
Ershad, Hussain Mohammad, 84

F

Faridpur, 43
Fatemi, Lt. Col., 73, 75–6, 86
Feni, 81, 85
France, 38
Frontier Force Regiment, 88

G

General Headquarters, 1, 2, 7, 9, 22, 24–27, 30, 38, 42, 47, 65, 66, 74, 93, 94
Germany, 38
Ghoraghat, 43
Government of East Pakistan, 13, 57
Government of India, 13
Government of Pakistan, 2, 4

H

Haq, Ziaul, 105
Haque, Maulvi Fazlul, 104
Hasina, Sheikh, 105
Hassan, Lieutenant General Gul, 7, 22, 25, 95
Headquarters 4 Corps, 1, 8
Headquarters 1 Corps, 9
Hossain, Dr Kamal, 33
Hotel Purbani, 49
Hussain, Major Mohammad, 90
Hussainiwala, 98

I

Imperial Defence College, 7
Inam-ul-Haque, Air Commodore, 69

INDEX

India, 8, 10, 13, 27, 48, 64, 67, 74, 79, 92, 97, 102–104, 110
Indian Border Security Force(s), 83, 92
Industrial Development Bank, 109
Intelligence Bureau (IB), 21
Inter-Continental Hotel, 72
Inter-Services Intelligence (ISI), 21
Iran, 31, 32
Ishurdi, 92
Islamabad, 109

J

Jagan Nath Hall, 18, 46
Janjua, Lt. Col., 73, 76
Janjua, Maj. Gen. Eftikhar Khan, 74, 75
Jessore, 9, 10, 15, 22, 24, 25, 68, 76, 77, 78, 82, 83, 92, 98
Jinnah, Mohammad Ali, 104
Joydebpur, 68, 75, 78

K

Kala Chand, 19, 20, 80, 95, 96
Kaptai Road, 88, 89
Karachi, 42, 53, 56, 57, 92, 96, 107, 109
Khan, Abdus Sabur, 10, 28
Khan, Air Marshal Asghar, 4, 99
Khan, Brigadier Ghulam Jilani, 52, 71, 99
Khan, Brigadier Mohammad Rahim, 7, 95–97, 99
Khan, Colonel Saadullah, 61, 76
Khan, Field Marshal Mohammad Ayub, 2–5, 7–9, 12, 13, 109
Khan, General Abdul Hamid, 22, 26, 41, 67, 69, 70
Khan, General Aga Mohammad Yahya, 7–9, 14, 22, 23, 29, 30, 34, 38, 41, 47, 48, 50, 56, 63, 64, 70, 100–102
Khan, General Yaqub, 7, 18, 23, 25, 27, 32, 52, 55–58, 64, 65, 70

Khan, Governor Abdul Monem Khan, 5
Khan, Liaquat Ali, 104
Khan, Lt. Col. Z.A., 81, 82
Khan, Lt. Gen Tikka, 9, 64–67, 69, 70, 76, 90, 93–95, 97
Khan, Maj. Gen. Mohammad Akbar, 21
Khan, Maj. Gen. Rahim, 7, 95–97, 99
Khan, Maj. Gen. Rao Farman Ali, 19, 20, 52, 55, 56, 57, 64, 66, 70, 71, 73, 76, 80, 96
Khan, Major Munawwar, 61
Khan, Maulana Akram, 93
Khan, Prince Karim Aga, 31
Khan, Wali, 100
Kharian, 67
Khulna, 9, 10, 36, 43, 83, 92, 109

L

Lahore, 5, 7, 9, 11, 38, 81–83, 96, 104
Lal Monirhat airfield, 83
Legal Framework Order, 31, 35 (n.2)

M

Maghreb, 8
Malik, Brigadier Abdullah, 83, 90
Malik, General Ihsan, 97
Malik, Lt. Col. Sarfaraz, 76, 83
Malik, Lt. Col. Yaqub, 75
Mandalpara, 92
Mangla, 9
Manora Hill, 89
Masood, Air Commodore, 51–52, 69
Meena Bazaar, 16, 17
Mitha, Maj. Gen. A.O., 87–90
Mohammad, Malik Sher, 90
Mohammedpur, 17
Mozumdar, Brigadier M.R., 74, 75
Mujahideen, 103
Mukti Bahini, 93
Multan, 1
Mumtaz, Commodore, 85

INDEX

Musharraf, Major Khalid, 84
Mushtaq, Major, 98
Muzaffaruddin, Maj. Gen., 9, 13, 14, 18
Mymensingh, 34, 43, 91

N

National Assembly, 34, 40–43, 48, 50; seats, 30, 31; session, 74
Naval Communication Centre, Tiger Pass, 85, 86, 89
Nawab Sirajuddaulah, 104
Nepal, 31, 38
Niazi, Lt. Gen. A.A.K., 95–99
Nilfamari, 92
North Bengal, 26, 90, 91, 107
North West Frontier Province, 95

O

One Unit, 35 (n.2)
Operation Blitz, 42, 43, 52
Operation Searchlight, 18, 73, 74, 76, 78, 79, 78–99
Osmani, Colonel M.A.G., 93

P

Pabna, 43, 83, 92
Padhrar, 90
Padma river, 91
Pakistan International Airlines (PIA), 51, 67
Pakistan Military Academy, Kakul, 88, 93
Pakistan Navy, 18, 89, 102
Pakistan People's Party (PPP), 40
Pakistan Resolution, 104
Paltan Maidan, 29, 49, 53
Parbatipur, 92
Pathan(s), 24, 55
Patuakhali, 38
Peelkhana, 79, 82

Peerzada, Lt. Gen. S.G.M.M., 53, 55, 57, 71
Philippines, 8
Punjabi(s), 5, 6, 10, 15, 24, 33, 37, 54, 83, 101, 108

Q

Qadir, Air Vice Marshal, 50
Qayyum, Brigadier Mian Abdul, 50
Qayyum, Colonel Abdul, 93
Quaid-i-Azam, 49, 104
Quetta, 1, 2, 42, 67, 91
Qureshi, Lt. Col. Hakim Arshad, 84

R

Radio Pakistan, 67
Rahman, Ataur, 17
Rahman, Lt. Gen. M. Attiqur, 1, 9
Rahman, Sheikh Mujibur, 10, 13–15, 28–30, 32–34, 39–41, 43, 48–51, 54, 56–63, 70, 72, 79, 81, 82, 92, 100–102
Raja, Rafia, 8, 55
Raja, Rubina, 81, 82
Rajarbagh, 79, 82
Rajshahi, 25, 76–78, 83, 92, 109
Ramna Race Course, 41, 59, 62
Rangoon, 51, 97
Rangpur, 26, 68, 76, 78, 83, 84, 90, 92
Rann of Kutch, 64
Rawalpindi, 3, 5, 7, 14, 24, 25, 38, 52, 57, 58, 90, 93
Reserve Police, 79, 82; Lines, 89
Riza, Maj. Gen. Shaukat, 67, 95
Roy, Raja Tridiv, 34

S

Saidpur, 26, 78, 84, 90
Shafi, Brigadier Iqbal, 73, 75, 76, 81, 85, 86
Shafi-ul-Azam, 53, 58

INDEX

Shah, Lt. Col. Syed Akabar Hussain, 17, 25
Shah, Lt. Gen. Riaz Hussain, 91
Shah, Maj. Gen. Nazar Hussain, 67, 95
Shah, Reza, 31
Shahpur, Lt. Col., 88
Shariff, Maj. Gen. Mohammad, 6
Shigri, Colonel, 73, 76
Sialkot, 25, 64
Singapore, 38
Six Points, 14, 28, 40, 101
Sobhan, Rehman, 33, 43, 44, 62
Sonar Bangla, 12, 14, 28, 101
Staff College, Quetta, 1, 3, 6, 7
State Bank of Pakistan, 53, 67
Subramanyam, 79
Suleman, Lt. Col., 87, 88
Syed, G.M., 100
Syed, Lt. Col. Saghir Hussain, 84
Sylhet, 31, 37, 68, 76, 78, 81, 83, 84

T

Taj, Lt. Col. Mohammad, 61
Tangail, 43, 91
Tashkent Declaration, 4
Thakurgaon, 26, 90

U

United States of America (USA), 37
Urdu, 6, 98, 105
United Pakistan, 5, 40, 104
Umar, General Ghulam, 14, 15

W

Wagah, 98
Wasiuddin, Lt. Gen. Khwaja, 26
West Bengal, 10
West Pakistan Army of Occupation, 17
West Pakistan, 5, 8, 11, 13, 14, 20, 23, 31, 40, 51, 54, 55, 63, 67, 71, 72, 88, 90, 93–95, 100, 101, 106–108; officer(s), 76, 84, 94, troops, 15, 16, 24, 74, 75
West Pakistani(s), 5, 6, 11, 16, 17, 53, 55, 69, 81, 84, 101, 105

Y

Yaqub, Lt. Col. Mohammed, 75

Z

Zia, Khaleda, 105
Zia-ur-Rahman, 76, 85, 88